Travellers Wine Guide

Italy

To Jane,
whom I met in Italy over a glass of Barolo

Travellers Wine Guide

Italy

Stephen Hobley

Photographs by Francesco Venturi

WAYMARK

The *Travellers Wines Guides*
were conceived and produced by
Philip Clark Limited
53 Calton Avenue, London SE21 7DF, UK

Designed by Keith Faulkner Publishing
Limited

Edited by Ros Mair

Photographs by Francesco Venturi
(except where otherwise credited)

Maps by Andrew Green and Simon Green

Published in Great Britain by
Waymark Publications, an imprint of
the Automobile Association, Fanum House,
Basingstoke, Hampshire RG21 2EA

© Philip Clark Limited, 1990
First published 1990

ISBN 0 86145 764 1

Phototypeset in Great Britain by
Input Typesetting Limited

Colour reproduction in Singapore by
Columbia Offset Limited

Printed and bound in Hong Kong

ACKNOWLEDGEMENTS

The author and publisher would particularly like to thank the following for their help in the preparation of this book: Mara Baldassari and Angelo Rossi of Comitato Vitivinicolo Trentino; Albano Bidasio of Consorzio Tutela Denominazione Vini D.O.C. Collio; Lina Carpo of Regione Piemonte, Assessorato all' Agricoltura; Richard Hobson of Italian Wine Agencies, London; Luciana Lynch; Maddalena Mazzeschi of Consorzio del Vino Nobile di Montalcino; Leonardo Montemiglio and Joanne Doherty of the Italian Trade Centre, London; Rolando Spadini of Co-operativa Monte Schiavo; Wine Buyers Guides Ltd.

PHOTO CREDITS

Maureen Ashley M.W. 129
Azienda Agricola Contucci 97
Casa Vinicola Collavini 66
Casa Vinicola Umberto Fiore 32
Casa Vinicola Roberto Kechler von Schwandorf 73
Cinzano Museum 31
Co-operativa Monte Schiavo 108
Co-operativa Locorotondo 115
Distilleria C. Bocchino 17
Faganello Zota 44/45
Italian Trade Centre, London 78
Tom O'Toole 12
C. Penna (Bava Collection) 18
Co-operativa Produttori del Barbaresco 37
Zefa Picture Library 40/41, 43, 133

Contents

How to Use this Book

There are several books on Italian wine that provide information on what to buy at home. This one is different. It is primarily intended to help you track down the fine wines that you can find in Italy itself.

This book aims to give the reader a recommended itinerary from one place of wine importance to another. It is not intended primarily as a cultural guide, but assumes that the reader will be interested in outstanding historic monuments and museums on the way.

The itineraries are, of course, in no way obligatory, and deviation from the sequence of visits suggested does not matter at all.

The main text describes areas to go to – for example the Langhe in Piedmont, the Franciacorta in Lombardy, and Chianti Classico in Tuscany – rather than individual wine producers to visit (except where the producer is exceptionally important or where space has permitted).

More often, the information about individual wine producers, wine shops and wine exhibitions is to be found in the information panels by the side of the main text. All the producers – and shops – detailed in these panels are recommended for the quality of their wines, but the list is, of course, by no means fully comprehensive. Wine to be tasted will vary from the honestly cheap and cheerful to the expensive and carefully crafted.

The information panels

The tinted panels which accompany the text of this tour through Italy will provide you with information which should be helpful when visiting a winery. The symbols used

(see the explanatory panel on the right) let you know what to expect.

Most wine companies offer tours on the tacit assumption that a small purchase at least will be made. Visits to a winery (see page 14) can be an education and a great pleasure; a real interest is always rewarded.

Enoteche

The word *Enoteca* (plural *Enoteche*) is used in Italy in two senses:

1. *Public Wine Exhibition*
These exhibitions are sponsored by local government or by a winemakers' *Consorzio*, and serve an educational, non-profit-making purpose.

Piedmont is particularly rich in this type of Enoteca. Most of them are sited in old castles and fortresses (see pages 22–23). Siena has the only permanent National Enoteca (see page 93).

All these Enoteche are listed in the information panels that accompany the text of this book, together with their opening hours. Most of them offer tastings as well and some of them have guided tours, which must be booked in advance.

2. *Wine shops*
Many commercial wine shops are also listed in this book. Some also serve wine by the glass at their own bar together with snacks. This can be a good way of getting to know about the wines of an area at a very modest cost, and is an excellent way of choosing and buying a bottle or two to take away with you.

Opening hours are usually the same as for any shop, though an Enoteca which provides tastings will sometimes be open late into the evening. Members of the Vinarius group are particularly good.

Information panel symbols

EP *Enoteca pubblica* local government-sponsored wine exhibition centre, sometimes including museum and restaurant

ER *Enoteca regionale* regional wine exhibition centre, the most important type of Enoteca pubblica

E English spoken
G German spoken
Fr French spoken
Sp Spanish spoken
TF tastings are free
TP tastings must be paid for
WS wine for sale
T booking required

Many of the entries conclude with additional points of interest.

Foreword

It was a chance encounter during an afternoon's exploration in northern Italy some years ago that brought me into the world of Italian wine. I was exploring the countryside of Piedmont in a leisurely fashion one weekend when I saw a signpost to Barolo. The name was already familiar to me, since I was working in Turin at the time and had often heard of this wine. The signpost struck a chord: maybe there was something of interest to see.

I was exceptionally fortunate. That weekend was the occasion of the official presentation in the castle of Barolo of the 1979 vintage. For the sum of 5,000 *lire* the visitor could taste all the 70 or so Barolos on display in the castle. The combination was enchanting – the highest quality Italian wine presented in a historic castle in one of the prettiest parts of Italy. I have been addicted ever since, and I still regard Barolo as the finest wine in the world.

Since that visit to Barolo I have been fortunate enough to be able to indulge my passion for Italian wine as part of my work. But it doesn't take long to discover that even if one has nothing to do with the wine world at all, most Italian wine producers are happy to spend hours talking to anyone who expresses an intelligent interest. Visiting wine producers in their wineries, talking about top class wines in specialist wine shops, selecting some interesting bottles from an Enoteca – these are pleasurable activities open to anyone who has just a little knowledge of wine already. If nothing else, wine is an extremely useful conversation piece; just by talking about wine to an Italian you begin to understand something about him, about his environment and about his culture. And no Italian can resist talking about the wine of his home town or province. Visit the cellars. Taste the marvellous wines of Italy.

Buon viaggio, and *buon divertimento*!

Stephen Hobley

Introduction _____

Italy has never lacked style. Lamborghini and Ferrari, Gucci and Armani – these are all internationally revered names. The Italian sense of style and the Italian way of living are generally much admired. And Italian food and the Mediterranean diet have made an impact worldwide.

But strangely enough, to many people Italy's food is more immediately appealing than the wine. Parmesan is better known than Pinot Bianco, Mozzarella has more cachet than Asti Spumante, Parma ham is in a different league to its traditional accompaniment, Lambrusco. The very names – Chianti, Soave, Frascati and Lambrusco – tend to conjure up the image of something cheap and cheerful with little to do with the world of Italian style or fashion.

In fact, however, the Italians produce some of the best wines in the world, some of the most stylish and some of the most refined. The quickest way to discover this world of fine wines is to travel in Italy, stop, look, visit and taste.

Italy is the world's largest producer of wine. But only about 10 per cent of wine production has the D.O.C. status (see pages 10–11). This 10 per cent represents those dedicated wine-makers who produce wine of ever-increasing quality and who range in size from the one man *vignaiolo* to the mighty wine producers. This book is largely about visiting their wineries.

Quality first
It is now very rare to come across a badly-made bottle of Italian wine. You may not like the style of the wine, but the greatest change in the last 15 or 20 years has been the introduction of modern technology in wine-making to the virtual elimination of faulty wine. In practice this has meant most for white wine production. Soave, Frascati and Verdicchio are now a positive pleasure to drink. They are crisp, clean and fruity wines, perfect for summer drinking.

Another aspect of the perfection of the wine technician's art is that it is now possible to tailor new wines to new markets. In Tuscany, for example, new whites and new red wines have been introduced by the marketing people to appeal to the new generation of wine drinkers. Galestro and Sarmento have no tradition, but they are inoffensive and very successful.

Producers are constantly striving to reconcile the demands of the market with the desire to make wines of increasing quality. Look out for the current bandwagons: ageing in small oak casks (*barriques*) – this lends a vanilla taste to the wine and makes it more 'international'; the rediscovery of local grape varieties; the introduction of international grape varieties – Cabernet Sauvignon and Chardonnay, for example; and the increase in sales of sparkling wine. There has never been a more exciting time to discover Italian wine.

NORTH CENTRAL ITALY

Bolzano

Trento

FRIULI-VENEZIA GIULIA

VENETO

Aosta

Milan

Trieste

Venice

Turin

Verona

Genoa

Bologna

VIA EMILIA

NORTH-WEST ITALY

Florence

Ancona

TUSCANY

Siena

Perugia

Pescara

L'Aquila

Rome

Campobasso

ADRIATIC COAST

CENTRAL ITALY

Bari

Naples

SARDINIA

Potenza

Lecce

MEDITERRANEAN COAST

Cagliari

Catanzaro

Palermo

SICILY

The Classification of Wines

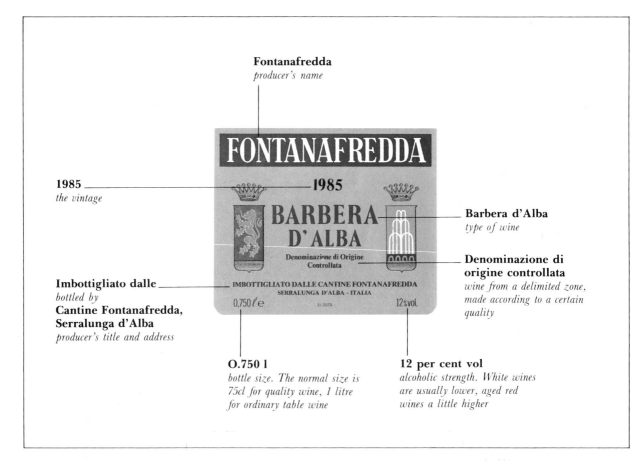

Fontanafredda
producer's name

1985
the vintage

Imbottigliato dalle
bottled by
**Cantine Fontanafredda,
Serralunga d'Alba**
producer's title and address

Barbera d'Alba
type of wine

**Denominazione di
origine controllata**
*wine from a delimited zone,
made according to a certain
quality*

O.750 l
*bottle size. The normal size is
75cl for quality wine, 1 litre
for ordinary table wine*

12 per cent vol
*alcoholic strength. White wines
are usually lower, aged red
wines a little higher*

Reading the label

Reading the label is not difficult and it gives valuable clues to the quality of wine in the bottle. Ultimately, the producer's name is more important than any labelling, but a few basic phrases help determine the wine's real potential.

Denominazione di Origine Controllata (D.O.C.):

literally, the origin of this wine is guaranteed. There are over 450 D.O.C. wines, all with their geographic provenance and grape composition enshrined by law. D.O.C. legislates only for a minimum quality, but it guarantees the *tipicità*, the typical characteristics of the wine.

Denominazione di Origine Controllata e Garantita (D.O.C.G.):

a refinement of the D.O.C., enacted in 1984 in order to impose a stricter quality control on a limited number of top wines. Brunello, Vino Nobile, Barolo, Barbaresco and Chianti are the D.O.C.G. reds; the only white is Albana di Romagna.

Vino con Indicazione Geografica:

similar to French *Vin de Pays*. Honest and typical local wine.

Vino da Tavola:

any wine that does not conform to D.O.C. regulations. There are several types: cheap, true table wines, *vino da pasto*; the mid-price, upmarket commercial wines,

such as Galestro and Sarmento; the expensive sort – designer wines, such as Tignanello, or Solaia (see label shown top right).

Wine types

Classico: from the heartland of the traditional production area. By implication (and usually in fact) better than others in the region.

Superiore: with slightly higher alcohol and, for reds, aged longer.

Riserva: aged much longer, but not as long as *riserva speciale*. This is used of wines such as Barolo and Barbaresco, wines to be laid down.

Spumante: sparkling wines, not usually made by the champagne method unless labelled *metodo classico* or *metodo champenois*.

Vigna or *Vigneti*: a single vineyard indication (as on the Vigneti Casterna label, right), implying a higher quality.

Vino novello: the same idea as Beaujolais Nouveau; new wine, to be drunk as young as possible.

Coltivazione biologica: organic wine. No chemical herbicides, *diserbanti* (see label, right).

Types of producers

Tenuta, Castello, Podere, Fattoria: traditional agricultural estates more or less devoted to wine production.

Azienda Agricola: a wine estate producing its own grapes. It will generally consider itself superior to the following:

Casa Vinicola: wine-makers using bought in grapes. They will argue that by buying in grapes they control what they get with greater accuracy.

Co-operativa: a co-operative (see also page 14).

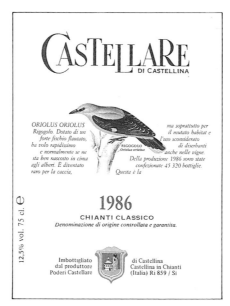

Solaia (above) is an upmarket wine made by Antinori, a leading Italian producer, but it still ranks as a Vino da Tavola. V.I.D.E. (top left) is a voluntary quality control association label that gives its authorization to approved wines. Vigneti Casterna (centre left) is a D.O.C. wine, a single-vineyard Valpolicella. Castellare (bottom left) declares its conservation interests on its labels – no herbicides are used in its vineyards. Neck labels with Consorzio symbols (below) are issued by the Consorzios to indicate that a wine has met with their minimum standards of wine production.

11

Travelling in Italy

Travelling by car

Some practical points:

* you must carry your driving licence and log book with you in the car; there is a fixed-penalty fine for not doing so. On-the-spot fines are applicable for traffic offences.
* the use of a warning triangle is compulsory in the case of an accident or breakdown. Failure to use one will incur a fine.
* petrol and motorway coupon schemes mean that 15% discount vouchers may be purchased in the U.K. if you intend driving a G.B. registered car in Italy.
* the purchase of petrol coupons also entitles the holder to emergency on-the-spot roadside assistance free of charge. Help can be summoned by dialling 116 on normal roads and otherwise by using the motorway emergency telephones. Any additional services must be paid for.
* Italians tend to drive fast and rely on their brakes. Rome has the worst traffic problems: the Via Emilia is the most dangerous road.

Northern Italian vineyards. Steep mountain slopes often make laborious work for the vine-grower. These terraced vineyards are in the hills of the Alto Adige, some 600 metres above Bolzano.

Southern Italian vineyards, set in a parched landscape, mainly produce grapes that give a characteristic 'baked' flavour to the wines.

* traffic lights are often left flashing amber throughout the night; you can always cross them, but beware of other cars.
* a car will flash its lights at another to warn the other car of its approach.
* in case of breakdown dial 116 at the nearest telephone box; the operator will inform the nearest A.C.I. (Automobile Club d'Italia) office of your needs.

Drinking and driving
The combination of car travel and visiting wineries means that the driver must be very aware of what he or she drinks. This book is not intended to encourage drinking and driving in any way. Italian drink/drive penalties are severe.

Travelling by train
The Italian railway is well subsidized, so fares are relatively inexpensive. But bear in mind these practical points:

* leave enough time to queue for a ticket. Subsidized fares mean that the railways are used by everyone.
* it is not true that Italian trains are usually late; long distance expresses sometimes are, but *rapido* and local trains are usually on time.
* there are five classes of train:
T.E.E. First class only, international trains. A special supplement is payable and seat reservation is obligatory.
Rapido Fast inter-city trains. A supplement (about 30 per cent) is payable. In some *rapido* trains seat reservation is obligatory.
Espresso Long distance trains, but not as comfortable or reliable as the *rapido*.
Diretto Stops at most stations.
Locale Stops at every station.

Travelling by air
There is an extensive internal air service in Italy. It saves time, but is not cheap.

SPEED LIMITS
Urban areas 50kph/31mph
Normal roads 80-110kph/50-68mph
Motorways 90-140kph/56-87mph (depending on size of engine)

Motoring organizations
In Italy there are two major motoring organizations:
A.C.I. (Automobile Club d'Italia), Via Marsala, 00185 Roma. Tel: 06 49981
T.C.I. (Touring Club Italiano), Corso Italia 10, 20122 Milano. Tel: 02 85261.

Maps
The most useful detailed driving maps are the 1:200,000 series produced by the Touring Club of Italy, the T.C.I.

General information
In the U.K., consult the Italian State Tourist Office, 1 Princes Street, London W1R 8AY. Tel: 01–408 1254: in the U.S., the Italian Government Travel Office, 630 Fifth Avenue, New York, N.Y. 10036. Tel: 212 245–4822.

Visiting a Winery

Organizing visits

The principal Consorzios
(wine promotional bodies),
usually willing to help
organize visits to their
members, are as follows.
(Full addresses appear at
the end of each chapter.)
Piedmont Asti Spumante;
Barolo and Barbaresco.
Lombardy Vini D.O.C.
Valtellina; Vini D.O.C.
Oltrepò Pavese; Vini
D.O.C. Bresciani.
Trentino Comitato
Vitivinicolo Trentino.
Veneto Vini D.O.C. Colli
Euganei; Associazione
Consorzi Vini D.O.C.
Vicentini; Bardolino; Vini
D.O.C. Lison Pramaggiore;
Prosecco; Vini D.O.C.
Piave.
Friuli-Venezia Giulia
Vini D.O.C. Collio; Vini
D.O.C. Grave del Friuli.
Emilia Romagna
Lambrusco di Modena;
Ente Tutela dei Vini
Romagnoli.
Marche Ente Sviluppo
nelle Marche.
Lazio Frascati.
Tuscany Chianti Putto;
Chianti Gallo Nero; Rosso
delle Colline Lucchesi;
Montecarlo; Vini di
Montalcino; Vino Nobile di
Montepulciano.
Umbria Orvieto Classico e
Orvieto.
Sicily Marsala.

Booking a visit

Most wineries require some notice of
an impending visit, for practical
reasons. *In extremis*, however, if you
arrive without warning and express
interest you will find Italians never
less than courteous and always
willing to help you if possible.

Booking can be made by telephone
or by letter. It is sometimes sufficient
to express interest, but most wineries
accept visitors on the understanding
that some purchase will be made,
however small.

Types of visit

Co-operatives These vary
considerably in size and outlook. In
general, it is those that are proud of
their wines, and keen to show that
being a co-operative is no handicap
to making good wines, that are most
ready to welcome foreign visitors.
Some co-operatives, however,
concentrate solely on bulk wine for
local consumption and are less
interested in visitors.
Large private companies The
grandest companies, the Antinoris

and Ruffinos of the Italian wine
world, will have public relations
departments, but these are not
generally orientated towards the
public. When arranging your visits,
it is often best to contact the
individual winery rather than depend
on the main office. Ruffino, in fact,
accepts visits from the general public;
Antinori does not.
Small private companies These are
often the most rewarding to visit.
The wine producer is often also the
owner of the company, although he
will probably have a consultant wine
expert (an oenologist) for the
technical aspects of wine-making.
Many are total enthusiasts who are
dedicated to promoting their wines.
Like most enthusiasts, they are
fascinating to talk to on their subject.
Enoteche Enoteche means 'places of
wine'. Two types are mentioned in
this book (see page 6).
1 'Public Exhibition and/or Tasting
Centre' – usually run by local
government. The general purpose is
educational. Booking may be
necessary for a guided tour.
2 The equivalent of a 'Specialist
Wine Shop' – a commercial
enterprise. Like any shop, booking is
not necessary and tasting is not
usually offered.

Tasting wine

It is very helpful to take notes when
you taste wine, so that you can build
up a sort of reference system, and
thus more easily compare one wine
with another tasted some time before.
It is useful to examine at least three
aspects of the wine:
Colour A light white is lighter in
colour than a heavier white. A young
red is brighter than an older red.
Nose Much of the taste of a wine can

be predicted from its smell. The perfume of the wine itself is part of the sensory pleasure of drinking.

Taste Does the wine balance the taste of the grape with the tannin (in red wines) or with the alcohol and the acidity? Is there a particular aftertaste to the wine?

Don't forget though that wine is to be enjoyed. If you like it, say so, drink it, and find some more.

The process of wine-making

White wines

1 Red (or white) grapes are broken away from their stems by machine.
2 A press crushes the grapes to extract the juice. This is separated from the skins and pumped into a fermentation vat (usually of stainless steel, and equipped for temperature control).
3 Fermentation ends. Sweet wine results when it is stopped before all the sugar in the grapes turns into alcohol. Vice-versa for dry wine.
4 When fermentation is complete and the wine has been drained (racked) off the sediment (lees) and clarified (fined), it is stored in large vats (often made of glass-lined concrete) until bottling.

Red wines

1 After crushing and de-stemming, the grapes are put into a vat to ferment.
2 Fermentation lasts until the sugar is used up, about a fortnight.
3 Racking and fining, as for white wines, above.
4 The wine is aged: in stainless steel for light wine, large barrels for a heavier wine, small barrels (*barriques*) for special wines that require the vanilla flavours of wood.

Sparkling wines

The process of fermentation usually provides the bubbles. This can be done in the bottle itself (Champagne method), or in large tanks (Charmat method), after which the wine is racked and fined before bottling. Cheap sparkling wine is produced by adding carbon dioxide to an ordinary wine.

The wine-tasting room of Siena's Enoteca Italica, Italy's permanent National Wine Exhibition centre (see also page 93).

Grappa

CANELLI (Asti)
Distilleria C. Bocchino
Via G. B. Giuliani 30. Tel:
0141 8101 (Signor Salvi).
All year. Closed Aug. t. E.
Fr. TF. WS. Unique
museum of distillation.

**LIZZANO DI
ROVERETO** (Trento)
**Ernesto Barozzi
Distilleria Dante** Via
Isonzo 7. Tel: 0464 433713
(Signorina Daniela). All
year. t. TF. WS.

MARLENGO (Bolzano)
**Distilleria
Untherthurner** Via A.
Pattis 14. Tel: 0473 47186.
All year, weekdays
0830–1230, 1430–1830, and
Sat (a.m. only). T. G. TF.
WS.

MONTEGALDA
(Vicenza)
**Distilleria e Fabbrica
Liquori Fratelli Brunello**
Via Roi 27. Tel: 0444
636024. All year (but
preferably in Sept-Nov). t.
E. TF. WS.

MUSOTTO D'ALBA
(Cuneo)
Distilleria Santa Teresa
Case Sparse 35. Tel: 0173
33144 (Paolo Marolo).
Office hours. T. E. Fr. TF.
WS. Maximum 12 visitors
at a time.

PERCOTO (Udine)
Distilleria Nonino
Via Aquileia 104. Tel: 0432
676333 (Signora Panelli).
Weekdays and Sat a.m.
office hours. T.E.TF. WS.

Among the many spirits and digestifs
that come from Italy, Grappa is one
of the most maligned. Mention the
equivalent French product, Marc de
Bourgogne or Marc de Champagne,
and there are instant smiles of
recognition. But Grappa,
unfortunately, has a reputation as
tourists' firewater. True, it can be
undrinkable and in general it is wise
to avoid anything that is very cheap.
But it can also be a drink of the
highest sophistication. It is important
to understand that several different
types are available.

Grappa profile

Grappa is produced throughout the
hills and mountains of northern Italy
and Tuscany. It has humble origins,
since it is essentially the distillate of
grape-pressings discarded by the
wine-maker. Mobile stills used to be
trundled from farm to farm at harvest
time, transforming the waste of the
wine-making process into a high
alcohol spirit, good for keeping the
cold out in winter. Today the
traditional home-made Grappa of
the mountain farmer can still be

found, served in the local trattorias
in the Alps and the Dolomites. But
modern Grappa is usually the widely
available brands, such as Grappa
Julia, Bocchino and Carpenè
Malvolti, sold in supermarkets, or the
upmarket, luxury product served in
smart restaurants.

Grappa types

There are four types of Grappa:
Grappa giovane This is young
Grappa, kept for about six months
in stainless steel after distillation,
thereby remaining clear in colour,
and concentrating the natural tastes
and fragrances of the distilled grape-
pressings.
Grappa invecchiata Aged Grappa,
kept for months or years in wood,
which gives it an amber colour and
makes it softer and smoother.
Grappa di mono vitigno The most
exclusive variety, made from a single
grape variety in order to enhance its
particular flavours. The strongly
perfumed varieties are very
attractive, especially to the palate
unfamiliar with Grappa. Grappa di
Moscato is a good example.

Grappa aromatizzata This is made with a herb or fruit flavouring and was traditionally used for medicinal purposes. Gentian-flavoured Grappa, they say, is a remedy for insomnia. In Alto Adige, especially, there is a tradition of making fruit-flavoured Schnapps: the Williams Pear is a favourite type.

The pioneers of Grappa

Grappa is the after-dinner drink of northern Italy and, after a recent revival, Tuscany. Producers can be visited in all those areas, but two in particular are outstanding.

The Nonino company, based in Friuli, were pioneers in the making of single-grape Grappas, the *Grappe di mono vitigno* described above. Giannola Nonino saw the possibility of selecting a grape variety for its particular virtues of taste and fragrance. Some of Nonino's finest Grappas are aged in cherry wood, a practice that started because cherry trees are plentiful in the area. Now the single-grape, cherry-wood aged Grappas of Nonino in their bulbous bottles are amongst the most sought after in Italy.

In Piedmont, the Bocchino firm has made Grappa since the turn of the century. Antonella Bocchino has rediscovered some of the traditional grape varieties of Piedmont to produce some very special single-grape Grappas. Neiret, Timuassa, Doux, and Vespolina d'Henry are some of the varieties.

Visit the company in Canelli to see their unique museum of distillation. The Bocchino brand is a commercial Grappa made from Moscato; Antonella's Grappas are much more expensive and are sold under the A.B. label.

The Bocchino Museum in Canelli preserves antique distillery equipment. The art of distillation is an ancient one, learned in part from the Arabs. The still used in the process is known as an 'alambic', a word derived from Arabic.

SCHIAVON (Vicenza)
Distilleria G. B. Poli
Via G. Marconi 10. Tel: 0444 665007 (Jacopo Poli, Teresa Parma). All year. T. E. Fr. TF. WS. Jacopo Poli is the founder of 'Distillatori Artigiani Vicentini', a group of craftsmen/distillers.

North-West Italy

North-west Italy comprises two areas of lesser importance in wine terms, Valle d'Aosta and Liguria, and one area which produces some of the finest wines in the world – Piedmont. Valle d'Aosta and Liguria are both mountainous areas, and they present extreme difficulties for the cultivation of vineyards. Wine in the Valle d'Aosta is produced with enormous effort from steeply sloping terraces which are clearly visible on both sides of the narrow Dora Baltea valley.

Similarly, in Liguria a boat trip around the headlands of the Cinque Terre or east of Savona towards the French border will reveal yet more precipitous vineyards in more hand-cultivated terraces. Unfortunately, the wines of both areas tend to be relatively expensive precisely because of these difficulties of production. But wine quality continues to rise in both regions despite a dramatic decline in viticulture in the last few years.

Each of the three regions has a distinct character. The Aostans have always regarded themselves as an independent mountain people, while the Ligurians have a proud seafaring heritage that goes back to the Genoese trade empire in the Middle

Fields and vineyards near the wine town of Asti create geometric patterns in shades of green.

Ages. But it was the Piedmontese who unified Italy, under King Victor Emmanuel (from 1861), and who still view the results with a somewhat amused detachment.

Piedmont is the Burgundy of Italy. It has a proud ducal past, its wines are produced on innumerable smallholdings according to ancient traditions, and few people claim to understand the *cru* (single vineyard) nature of its most famous wines, Barolo and Barbaresco. But even a lowly trattoria will produce a very drinkable opaque wine, normally one of the house reds: Dolcetto and Barbera. Their characteristic slight *pétillance* is not a sign of bad wine-making, but rather of how Italians like their young red wines. It is more difficult to find good white wines. Cortese di Gavi and Erbaluce di Caluso can be good. Gavi di Gavi has become very fashionable.

Also included in this section is a part of Lombardy: the sparkling wine producing area of Oltrepò Pavese.

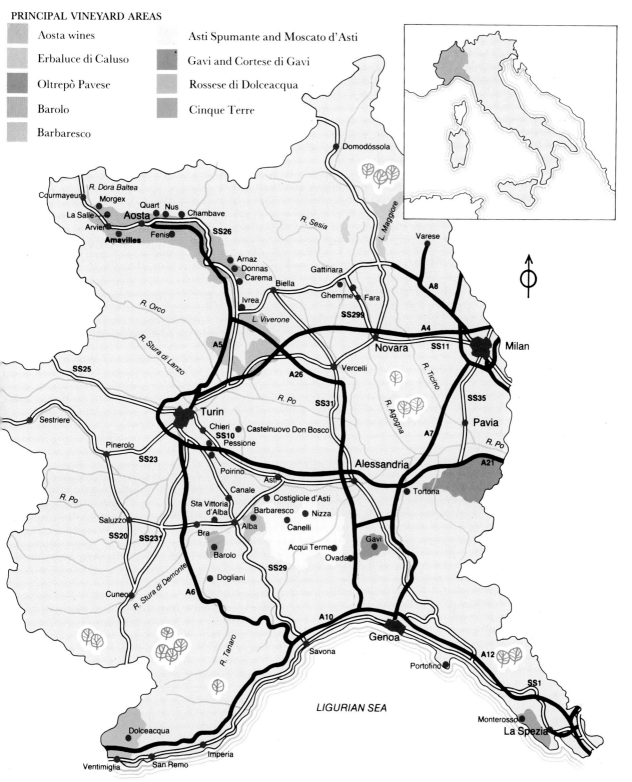

PRINCIPAL VINEYARD AREAS

- Aosta wines
- Erbaluce di Caluso
- Oltrepò Pavese
- Barolo
- Barbaresco
- Asti Spumante and Moscato d'Asti
- Gavi and Cortese di Gavi
- Rossese di Dolceacqua
- Cinque Terre

Valle d'Aosta

AOSTA
Enoteca Cave Valdotaine
Via De Tellier 9. Mon-Sat
0900–1230, 1500–1930.
Closed Mon a.m., and Oct
holidays.
Institut Agricol Régional
Reg. La Rochère 1a. Tel:
0165 553304 (Paolo
Bruchez). Weekdays and
Sat a.m. T. TF. WS. School
for local *vignerons* since 1949.

AYMAVILLES
Charrère Antoine et Fils
Fr. Moulin 33, Aymavilles.
Tel: 0165 902135
(Constantin Charrère).
May-Sept. T (minimum 4
visitors). Fr. TP. WS. Small
display of antique milling
machinery.

CHAMBAVE
Az. Agr. Voyat Ezio Via
Alberaz 13/15, Chambave.
Tel: 0166 46139 (Signor
Ezio Voyat). All year. T.
Fr. TF (with sale). WS.
Ancient cantina. Makes
the unusual *moscato passito
secco*.

CHARVENSOD
Viticoltore Aldo Perrier
Loc. Charvensod 76. Tel:
0165 34722. Apr-Oct. t. Fr.
TF. WS.

DONNAS
**Caves Co-operatives de
Donnas** Via Roma 97,
11020 Donnas. Tel: 0125
82096. All year. T. Fr. TF.
WS.

LA SALLE
**Cave du Vin Blanc de
Morgex et de La Salle** Via
Gerbollier 5, La Salle. Tel:
0165 861105 (Bruno Salice).
All year. T. Fr. TP. WS.

Since 1947 Valle d'Aosta has been an
autonomous region within Italy with
the same local government freedoms
as the similarly mountainous border
regions of Trentino and Alto Adige.
Signs in Aosta are usually bilingual
and the dialect of the local people is
an impenetrable mixture of Italian
and French that is more readily
understood by the mountain
dwellers on the French side of the
border than by other Italians.

Valle d'Aosta is well known to
skiers for its resorts at Courmayeur
and Cervinia and to naturalists for
the Gran Paradiso National Park. It
is not well known for its wine even in
Italy, but it has recently become the
subject of an experiment whereby, as
happens in France, the whole area
has been made into a geographical
appellation and all its quality wines
are now D.O.C. (for explanation, see
page 10). Considering the fact that
Valle d'Aosta is by far the smallest
producer of wines in Italy, and that
those wines which have survived the
pressures of modern economics
count amongst some of Italy's most
interesting rarities, this experiment
seems justified.

Aosta valley
The Aosta valley is famous for its
chain of castles leading down to the
Piedmontese border. There are 130
in all; some are now no more than
ruined watchtowers, others were
splendidly restored in the last
century. The castles of Issogne and
Fenis, both restored by the architect
of Turin's incredible *Borgo Medioevale*,
Alfredo d'Andrade, are most
attractive; the fortress of Bard is
forbidding. Fenis also has a museum
of local history, the *Museo
dell'Arredamento Valdostano*.

The wines
Some wines are made throughout the
valley. Gamay is a light quaffable
red made from the same grape as
Beaujolais. Müller-Thurgau is made
from the international grape of the
same name. The same applies to
Pinot Nero, but unusually it is also
possible to find this as a white wine.

La Valdigne
The narrow valley of the Valdigne
extends some 27km (17 miles) from
Mont Blanc until just before Avise.
The only vine that grows in this
area, an indigenous one called Blanc
de Morgex or Blanc di Valdigne, has
the useful qualities of being able to
survive at higher altitudes than other
vines and of being resistant to the
deadly disease phylloxera. The area
produces the wines Blanc de Morgex
and Blanc de la Salle, both good
white aperitif wines. The town of
Morgex is the commercial centre
and La Salle has a notable castle.

La Valle Centrale
This area extends from Avise to St
Vincent, where the road and the
Dora Baltea river suddenly plunge
southwards towards Piedmont.

About 16km (10 miles) further on
is the village of Arvier, with its
intriguingly named Enfer d'Arvier, a
light red wine with a pleasingly
bitter aftertaste.

Still on the SS26 and a few miles
after Aosta are the villages of Nus
and Chambave, which give their
names to two wines, which can be
either red or white. Chambave in its
white version is made from the
Moscato grape, and in its most prized
form can be made from partly dried
grapes and have a formidable
alcoholic content.

Torrette, the other particular D.O.C. wine of the Valle Centrale, is a dry, slightly bitter red wine made principally from the Petit Rouge, another of the grapes indigenous to the Valle d'Aosta.

La Bassa Valle

The 25km (15 miles) of the Bassa Valle extend from St Vincent to the border with Piedmont. The vineyard terraces cloak the valley slopes.

It is when one nears the border with Piedmont that the land of classic Nebbiolo-based wines begins with the red wines called Arnad-Montjovet and Donnas. These are made from the same grape that their heavier cousins Barolo and Barbaresco are made from, but they are not aged for so long and can be much subtler wines. They are also very difficult to find outside their own areas of production.

The steeply-terraced vineyards of the Valle d'Aosta are clearly visible both from the fast autostrada *and the winding* superstrada. *Viticulture is laborious and expensive.*

The Enoteche of Piedmont

ACQUI TERME
ER Palazzo Robellini. Tel: 0144 770274. Weekdays 1000–1200, 1500–1830. Closed Mon, Wed and Thurs a.m.s. TP. WS.

BARBARESCO
ER Via Torino 8a. Tel: 0173 635251. Wed, Thurs, Fri, 1500–1900, Sat and Sun 1000–1200, 1500–1800. Closed Mon and Tues. TP. WS. Selection of Barbaresco.

BAROLO
ER Castello Comunale. Tel: 0172 56277. 1000–1230, 1500–1830. Closed Thurs and Jan. Book for guided tasting. Museum of glasses. Library of Silvio Pellico. TP. WS.

COSTIGLIOLE D'ASTI
ER Castello di Costigliole. Tel: 0141 966015/966289. T. TP. WS. Restaurant.

GRINZANE CAVOUR
ER Castello di Grinzane. Tel: 0173 62159. Mon, Wed, Thurs, Fri 1000–1200, 1500–1800, Sat and Sun 0900–1300, 1430–1800. Closed Tues and Jan. Museum. TP. WS. Restaurant.

LA MORRA
Cantina Comunale
Palazzo Comunale. Tel: 0173 50887. Open Sat, Sun and (p.m.) Tues, Thurs. EP.

The castle of Barolo (see page 27 for a brief history) is one of the eight Piedmontese Enoteche. On display are over 100 different varieties of Barolo, Italy's 'King of Wines and Wine of Kings'. The castle also contains a hotel school and a museum.

The wine traveller in Piedmont is exceptionally fortunate. The Piedmontese regional government has long pursued a policy of encouraging wine tourism with the development of, so far, eight regional Enoteche and several regional Botteghe del Vino specifically designed for the purpose of informing the visitor about Piedmont's magnificent wines.

The difference between the two types of wine showplace is one of size and scope. An Enoteca will certainly display the wines of its area, but it will also often have a restaurant designed to serve complementary local foods and a museum of wine-making artefacts. The Bottega tends to be more modest, more specialized, and opens only at weekends. At Carema, for example, there is only the excellent wine of that name; at Canale there is only the new D.O.C. wine, Roero.

There is a double pleasure in visiting the Enoteche of Piedmont: they are all sited in monuments of historic interest that have been recently restored to serve as showcases for the local vinous heritage. Five are in castles, two are mere *palazzi*, the remaining Enoteca is in the deconsecrated church of San Donato in Barbaresco.

Grinzane Cavour

If there is time to visit only one of these Enoteche or Botteghe, the one that is obligatory is the Enoteca Regionale at Grinzane Cavour, near Alba. This is an imposing castle dating from the mid-13th century, which, as the name recalls, was once the property of the great statesman of the Risorgimento, Camillo Benso di Cavour. The prototype of the Enoteca system, it was opened in 1971 as the showplace for the best wines and Grappas of Piedmont. Its wine selection is controlled by the splendidly named and, on ceremonial occasions, splendidly robed 'Master Tasters of the Order of the Knights of the Truffle and the Wines of Alba'. It is an experience not to be missed to taste some of the finest wines in the world in the mediaeval setting of this hilltop castle. A restaurant within the castle serves Piedmontese specialities, and its museum has interesting historical displays on coopering, distilling, and truffle hunting.

Botteghe

There are at least two dozen Botteghe del Vino in Piedmont. More are being opened as small groups of wine-growers band together to take advantage of the growing public interest in genuine hand-made

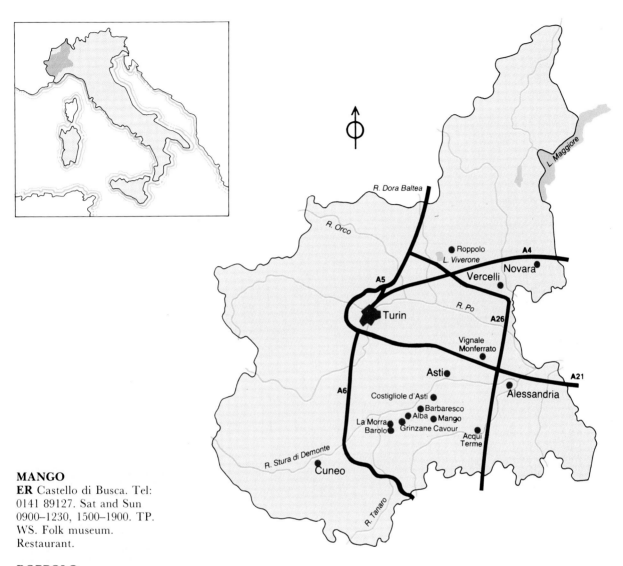

MANGO

ER Castello di Busca. Tel: 0141 89127. Sat and Sun 0900–1230, 1500–1900. TP. WS. Folk museum. Restaurant.

ROPPOLO

ER della Serra Castello di Roppolo. Tel: 0161 98501. 1500–1900. Closed Mon. TP. WS. Also hotel in castle.

VIGNALE MONFERRATO

ER Palazzo Callori. Tel: 0142 923243. Daily 0900–1200, 1500–1900. TP. WS. Restaurant. Deepest well in Piedmont (57 m/187 ft).

products of the countryside, of which wine is only one. An increasing nostalgia for the countryside, combined with interest in *agriturismo*, holidaying in the country rather than the traditional skiing or beach holidays, has created a greater willingness on the part of the wine-maker to exhibit his wines. (For more information on *agriturismo*, see page 98.)

Of the Botteghe perhaps the most interesting is the Cantina Comunale of La Morra, near Cuneo. This is only open at weekends and on Tuesday and Thursday afternoons, but it is in the heartland of Barolo production. You can find details of local vineyard walks, and La Morra itself is unique in having a statue not to a wine-maker but to *Il Vignaiolo*, the vine-grower.

Piedmont – South of Turin

The Royal Hunting Lodge at Stupinigi on the outskirts of Turin. Those who think of the city as mainly industrial are amazed by the range of its architectural masterpieces.

The major wine interest of north-west Italy lies in Piedmont. As its name suggests, it is found at the foot of mountains, indeed it is surrounded by mountains to the north and west, and its inhabitants are distinctly proud of their mixed French and Italian heritage. The charismatic soldier-general Garibaldi, who captured Sicily and Naples for the newly unified Italy was, after all, born in Nice when that city was still a part of the old Sardinian Kingdom, ruled by the Savoyard monarchy.

Piedmont might be more famous for its successful industries, FIAT and Olivetti; but for the wine lover it signifies the great Italian wines of Barolo and Barbaresco. In fact Piedmont is particularly rich in wine; it has no fewer than 35 D.O.C. wines and two D.O.C.G.s (for explanations, see page 10).

Wine routes

Six years ago the Piedmontese regional government began to plan a system of wine roads for the tourist. However, it seems as if the full *Strada del Vino* system will never be established: there are too many wines and their Denomination areas overlap too confusingly for the signposts ever to be comprehensive or comprehensible. The distinctive yellow signs that are already in place are now acknowledged as pointers that lead the motorist in the right general direction rather than providing a fixed wine itinerary. Following these signs will provide a pleasant drive in the country, but a detailed road map and a little wine knowledge are essential supplements. If a wine company sports the *Strada del Vino* logo outside its premises it is worth asking if a visit is possible, but the sign carries with it no obligation that the company should show the visitor around the premises.

One initiative that has succeeded is the establishment of regional Enoteche and local Botteghe del Vino (see pages 22–23). The following routes form a curve around Turin, a tour based on these excellent wine information centres.

Turin and its vicinity

Turin is often disparaged by Italians from outside Piedmont, and its ring-road system is successful enough for it to be bypassed as a matter of course by the car-borne traveller. But it has many attractions. This is the lovely arcaded city where Michael Caine was filmed in *The Italian Job*. It should be visited for its museums, palaces and churches, often built in a wonderfully extravagant Torinese Baroque style. It also has some of

the finest Liberty style buildings in Europe, dating around the turn of the century, and an Egyptology Museum second only to Cairo's.

Leaving Turin to the south-east by the SS10 to Chieri, a brief stop can be made at Superga, an extraordinary 18th-century basilica that looks out over the city and houses the Savoia Mausoleum.

Terra dei Santi

Chieri is rich in 15th-century churches (S. Domenico, S. Giorgio, the Duomo), and is a centre for the production of a traditional Piedmontese wine that is rarely seen abroad, Freisa. The name comes from its strawberry-like bouquet and in both its sweet and dry versions it is a good alternative to Lambrusco.

After Chieri a diversion to Pessione leads to the fascinating Martini & Rossi winery and museum. The most impressive exhibits are the carts used to transport barrels for the new vintage's wine, all marvellously carved with appropriate scenes of Bacchic revelry.

North-east of Chieri is Moncucco Torinese with its Bottega del Vino and associated Trattoria della Freisa. This specializes in Freisa and in Malvasia, which is most easily found as a sweet sparkling red, Malvasia di Castelnuovo Don Bosco. It makes an excellent aperitif.

The whole area is sometimes called the *Terra dei Santi* because of its associations with Turin's famous philanthropic priest Don Bosco, and the missionary S. Giuseppe Cafasso. The abbey of Vezzolano near Castelnuovo Don Bosco is worth visiting for its perfect Romanesque architecture and its setting in the midst of vineyards.

MONCUCCO
Bottega del Vino di Moncucco Via Masso 6. Tel: 0141 9874765. Closed Tues and Weds. EP. TP. WS. Also attached to restaurant, Trattoria del Freisa.

PESSIONE DI CHIERI
Museo Martini di Storia dell'Enologia (Martini Museum of the History of Oenology). Tel: 011 9470345. Mon-Fri 0800–1700. t. Guided visit. Model of Roman cellars, vineyard and cellar implements, antique glass, bottles, carved wine carts.

TURIN
Specialist wine shops:
Il Bottigliere Via S. Francesco da Paola 43. 0930–1330, 1400–1900. Closed Thurs, and Sun a.m.
Il Vinaio Via Cibrario 38. 0830–1300, 1500–2000. Closed Sun, and Wed p.m.
Renato Rabezzana Via Francesco d'Assisi 23. 0830–1300, 1530–1930. Closed Mon, and Sun a.m. Also wine-makers from S. Desiderio d'Asti.
Vini Selezionati Borio Via Buenos Aires 70. 0700–2000. Closed Sun. Specializes in Cascina Castlèt wines of Maria Borio.

Piedmont – Alba

ALBA
Museo Ratti dei Vini d'Alba Fraz. Annunziata. Tel: 0173 50185. T. Maps, prints, antiquarian objects.

BRA
Cantine Ascheri Giacomo Via Piumati 23. Tel: 0172 412394 (Matteo Ascheri). Open all year. t. E. G. Fr. TF. WS.

CANALE D'ALBA
Bottega del Vino del Roero Corso Torino 11. Tel: 0173 95057 (Roberto Damonte). Sat 1500–1900, Sun 0900–1200, 1500–1900. EP. T. TP. Mediaeval cellars, regional wines.

DOGLIANI
Bottega del Vino Palazzo Comunale. Tel: 0173 70107. Sun and holidays. EP. In former monastery.

NEIVE
Bottega dei Quattro Vini Palazzo Comunale. Tel: 0173 67110. Open weekends and holidays. EP.

Towards Alba

Alba is the capital of the Langhe, a wonderful area full of gently rolling hills with mediaeval castles and villages perched upon them. It is best visited in the autumn when truffles perfume the streets, the vines have turned russet colour and the new vintage froths in the vats.

Turin to Alba via Canale d'Alba

The SS29 passes through Poirino to Canale d'Alba, a town known for confectionery, but also for the Bottega del Vino del Roero. At present Roero D.O.C. means the red Nebbiolo wine of this left bank of the Tanaro, but the prestigious whites Arneis del Roero and Favorita are also exhibited at this Bottega.

From Canale d'Alba the SS29 passes over the Tanaro to Alba.

Alternatively, from Turin take the A6 *autostrada* for Savona, turning off for Bra, once a centre for Barolo producers, now better known for Baroque churches and its 15th-century town museum. Alba can

also be reached with a very short diversion to S. Vittoria d'Alba, the town with a secret, according to the story of the efforts of its inhabitants to hide their underground stores of wine from the occupying Germans. The Cinzano Museum nearby is also worth a visit.

The Alba zone

From Alba turn south to the land of Barolo, a triangular area with its points at Alba, Cherasco and Dogliani.

An essential visit is the Enoteca Regionale at Grinzane Cavour (see pages 22–23) to learn about Piedmontese wines, and truffles and, preferably, to consume both.

From Grinzane Cavour it is a short drive to La Morra, where the Bottega del Vino is located in the cellars of the Town Hall, the Palazzo Comunale. The Museo Ratti at the Abbazia

dell'Annunziata nearby displays a unique wine artefact collection.

From La Morra retrace your route to the road to Barolo, and its Enoteca, housed in a castle with a hotel school and a small museum. It displays Barolo from over a hundred producers. From 1250 to 1864 it was the home of the Falletti, and it was the last Marchesa, Giulia, who is credited with the creation of Barolo in the 19th century. The change she made was to vinify the wine so that it would be drier and age longer. Previously it had been a sweet wine to drink young.

Dolcetto and Barbaresco

From Barolo take the road to Dogliani, whose Bottega del Vino is devoted to one of Piedmont's great table wines, Dolcetto. The name derives from the sweetness only of the grapes and Dolcetto itself is a smooth robust red wine which has a slightly bitter aftertaste.

The return journey to Alba takes in typical picturesque villages of the Langhe. Stop at Serralunga d'Alba for its castle. Also worth seeing nearby is the winery of Fontanafredda, which is sited at the old royal hunting lodge where Victor Emmanuel II, first King of all Italy, kept his mistress 'La Bella Rosin'.

Barbaresco's Enoteca is sited in the deconsecrated church of San Donato and shows only Barbaresco, often said to be more refined than its cousin Barolo.

Close to Barbaresco is the hilltop town of Neive, an area for top quality Barbaresco. Its ancient Town Hall is the site of a Bottega del Vino which specializes in Barbera, Dolcetto, Moscato and, of course, Barbaresco. Every summer the town hosts a Festival of Wine Songs.

Vineyards encircle the wine town of Barbaresco, which lies north-east of Alba.

SERRALUNGA D'ALBA
Tenimenti di Barolo e Fontanafredda Via Alba 15. Tel: 0173 53161 (Signora M. Maiorano). Apr 1–Nov 30. T. E. G. Fr. TF. WS. Guided visits at weekends (in Italian).

S. VITTORIA D'ALBA
Cinzano Museum Tel: 0172 47041 (Signora Pastorino). Office hours. T. Antique glass, wine-making and distillery equipment.

Further addresses:
For the Enoteche of Barolo, Grinzane Cavour and Barbaresco, and the Bottega del Vino di La Morra, see pp.22–23. For other useful addresses, see pp.36–37.

Piedmont – Asti

From Costigliole d'Asti take the road to Nizza Monferrato, where there is the famous Bersano Museum with its collection of prints and documents dedicated to wine, dating from the 17th century.

Visit Cantine Duca d'Asti in nearby Calamandrana for an idea of what a modern but traditionally-minded wine producer can achieve. Try the experimental barrique-aged Barilot if possible.

Finally, when returning to Asti, take the road to Montegrosso d'Asti, which boasts a Bottega del Vino showing Barbera, Grignolino and Dolcetto.

ASTI
Bottega dei Vini Douja d'Or Expo Salone, Piazza Alfieri, Portici Pogliani. Tel: 0141 50067. Wed-Sun 1000–1230, 1600–2000. EP. Closed Mon, Tues. TP. WS.

CALAMANDRANA
Cantine Duca d'Asti di Michele Chiarlo. Tel: 0141 75231 (Roberto Bezzeto). All year. T. E. Fr. TF. WS.

CANELLI
Fratelli Gancia & C. Corso Libertà 16. Tel: 0141 8301 (Mauro Suani). Closed July 25–Aug 25 and Dec 20–Jan 10. T (by letter). E. G. Fr. TF. WS.

COSTIGLIOLE D'ASTI
Cascina Castlèt Strada Castelletto 6. Tel: 0141 966651 (Maria Borio / Gianni Bianco). All year. T. TF. WS.

MONTEGROSSO D'ASTI
Bottega del Vino Fraz. Vallumida 15. Tel: 0141 953052. EP. Open Sat, Sun and weekday hols.

South bank of the Tanaro
Continuing along the left bank of the Tanaro from Barbaresco, take the road to Costigliole d'Asti and the Alto Monferrato. Confusingly, the *Alto* is south of the *Basso* Monferrato, but the whole territory continues the range of hills in a crescent from the Langhe south of Turin to the Casalese east of Turin. The part to begin with is the triangular route to the south of the Tanaro, from Costigliole d'Asti to Nizza Monferrato, and from there to Asti.

The most important stop of all is the Enoteca Regionale in the white-painted castle of Costigliole d'Asti. Half the castle belongs to the *comune*. The other half is still private property and used to belong to the Contessa di Castiglione who became mistress to the French king Napoleon III. Only wines that come from the Asti territory, the Astigiana, and have been awarded the prestigious annual *Douja d'Or* prize, are exhibited here. An excellent restaurant serves local specialities in the state rooms on the *piano nobile*.

Asti
Asti itself possesses a cathedral which is the supreme example of Piedmontese Gothic architecture; it has an impressive art gallery and a museum of the Risorgimento. But above all its name is synonymous with sparkling wine. This is the headquarters of the National Association of Wine Tasters and Grappa Tasters and the wine confraternity *L'Ordine dei Cavalieri delle Terre di Asti e del Monferrato*.

Asti Spumante and Moscato
At Alba turn south on the SS29 and drive to the Valle Belbo. Between this valley and Acqui Terme are the principal vineyards for Asti Spumante and Moscato d'Asti. Asti Spumante is world famous and much misunderstood; it can have a dry finish as well as a sweet one and it makes an excellent celebration wine, not as a substitute for Champagne, but as an accompaniment to sweet cakes and puddings. Consuming the classic Italian Christmas cake or *panettone* is

inconceivable without a glass of Asti Spumante. Moscato d'Asti is only slightly *pétillant* and is a dessert wine for the connoisseur.

The Belbo valley has been made famous in the novels of the writer Cesare Pavese (1908–50). The Bottega del Vino at Quaranti d'Asti is especially worth a visit at the time of the festive Palio in Asti, a good opportunity to taste typical country foods like *ceci* (chickpeas) and *cotechino* (salami).

S. Giorgio Scarampi and Mango

There is another Bottega del Vino at San Giorgio Scarampi in the Val Bormida. It has its own restaurant (try the pasta *agnolotti* here) and specializes in Barbera, Moscato and Barbaresco. The Enoteca Regionale for the Moscato country is on the way from Alba to Santo Stefano at Mango. The square 17th-century castle in which it is sited dominates the town. It has a museum of country life and a restaurant, and each year it awards a prize for the best Christmas cake that must, naturally, have Moscato wine as one of its ingredients.

Vermouth

Following the valley north one arrives at Canelli, a centre for both Spumante and Vermouth. Of the well-known names, however, Martini is nearer Turin (see page 25), and Cinzano nearer Alba (see page 26). Gancia and Riccadonna are in Canelli. Other wines of the area include the rare dry white Furmentin and the sparkling red dessert wine Brachetto d'Acqui.

NIZZA MONFERRATO
Bersano, Antico Podere Conti della Cremosina, SpA Piazza Dante 21. Tel: 0131 721273 (Signora Maria Giovanna Calvi). Weekdays Apr-June, Sept-Oct 0900–1100, 1400–1700. T. E. Fr. Wine museum.

QUARANTI D'ASTI
Bottega del Vino di Quaranti
Via del Castello. Tel: 0141 77081. Daily 0800–1200, 1400–2000. EP. In the mediaeval priest's house of the church of S. Lorenzo.

Castello Gancia in Canelli. Gancia were the pioneers of Asti Spumante, once made in the bottle, like Champagne, but now made in steel tanks.

Piedmont – Monferrato

GRIGNOLINO
DEL MONFERRATO CASALESE
DENOMINAZIONE DI ORIGINE CONTROLLATA
1987

MESSO IN BOTTIGLIA DA *Franco-Fiorina* ALBA-ITALIA
75cl e   12%vol.

CERRO TANARO
Giorgio Carnevale srl
Via G. Trombetta 117. Tel:
0141 609115 (Alessandro
and Giorgio Carnevale).
All year. t. E. Fr. TF. WS.

COCCONATO D'ASTI
Cantine Bava Borgo
Stazione. Tel: 0141 907084
(Signor Bava). Open all
year. t. E. Fr. TF. WS.
Visit also old cellars and
exhibition centre of Casa
Brina nearby.

COSSANO BELBO
**Fratelli Martini Secondo
Luigi snc** Via Statale 6.
Tel: 0141 88242 (Gianni
Martini). March-Sept. T.
TF. WS. Minimum 5
visitors.

**CASALE
MONFERRATO**
**Az. Agr. Ermenegildo
Leporati** Strada Asti 29, S.
Germano Monferrato. Tel:
0142 55616 (Signora Teresa
Leporati). All year. t. E. Fr.
TF. WS.

The Basso Monferrato
From Asti go north to Portacomaro
in the Basso Monferrato. This is a
beautiful area of sleepy towns on
gentle hills, vineyards and woods,
lying to the south of the Po and from
the north of Asti to Canale
Monferrato. Cocconato d'Asti on its
western borders has a fine hilltop
view over the area and two good
restaurants, ideal for lunchtime.

Portacomaro has a Bottega del
Vino sited in a tower, all that
remains of the town's castle. It
specializes in Grignolino and, a
rarity indeed, Grappa di Grignolino.
Grignolino is a classic Piedmontese
wine that is much undervalued. It is
a light red wine with a bitter cherry-
stone twist to its finish that, in the
hands of the right producer, can be
superb. At present it suffers from its
reputation as a wine to be drunk
young; it is better aged a little.

From Portacomaro it is about
16km (10 miles) to Vignale with its
Enoteca Regionale in the Palazzo
Callori, specializing in Barbera and

Grignolino. Vignale has a 13th-
century church and a dance festival.

From Vignale go to Moncalvo,
another centre for Grignolino, which
is famous for its food; *bollito*, delicious
boiled meats, is a speciality. It is one
of the few towns in Piedmont to
retain its *Fiera del Bue Grasso*, a
festival day when a garlanded ox is
the centre of a procession.

Towards Casale the commonest
building stone is *tufo*. Blocks of this
soft material form the walls of farm
buildings, and conversely wine
cellars are excavated from it, the
famous *infernotti*. These are difficult
to visit because of continuing use, but
the Vignale Enoteca has a display of
photographs of the strangely chapel-
like underground wine stores.

Barbera
The other wine of this area is the fruit
of the most common of Piedmont's
vines, Barbera. It has long suffered
from over-production and the
lowering of the alcohol content in the
table wine market. Solutions so far
have been to emphasize two types of
Barbera, Barbera vivace (*pétillant*),
and Barbera storico (still), to vinify
it as a white wine and use it as
a base for Spumante. In the right
hands there is nothing wrong with
traditional Barbera – it is a good red
table wine with a pleasant bite to it.

The major local producers prefer
to make entirely new wines with
Barbera as a base, but using modern
techniques for lighter and fruitier
styles. Look for Rovetto, Barbesino
and Arengo, 'the first red wine made
to be drunk cool'. Verbesco is a
commercial white that should appeal
to those who like the Tuscan Galestro
– both are light fruity wines, good
for alcohol-conscious wine drinkers.

CASTAGNOLE MONFERRATO
Bottega del Ruchè Via Vittorio Emanuele 17. Tel: 0141 292173. Sat and Sun. EP. T (for group visits).

S. GIORGIO SCARAMPI
Bottega del Vino della Langa Astigiana 'Valle Bormida' Via Roma, S. Giorgio Scarampi. Tel: 0144 89230. Open Sun. T. TF.WS.EP.

PONZANO MONFERRATO
Az. Agr. Cassinis Castello di Salabue. Tel: 0141 927195 (Adriana Cassinis). Sat and Sun 1000–1800. EP. t. TP. WS.

PORTACOMARO D'ASTI
Bottega del Vino di Grignolino Torre del Recetto. Tel: 0141 202666. March-Oct, Thurs 1500–1930, Sat and festivals 0900–1230, 1500–1930. EP.

VIGNALE MONFERRATO
Az. Agr. Nuova Cappelletta Loc. Cà Cappelletta 9. Tel: 0142 923135 (Eugenio Arzani). All year Mon-Fri 0830–1000, 1400–1800. T E. TF. WS.
Poderi Bricco Mondalino Loc. Bricco Mondalino. Tel: 0142 923204 (Mauro Gaudio). All year. E. TF. WS. Tasting in own tavernetta.

An old-fashioned manual corking machine for bottles of Asti Spumante. This one is on display in the Cinzano Museum at S. Vittoria d'Alba (see page 27 for visiting details).

Piedmont – the North-East

The distinctive terraces with their stone *topioni* pillars signal the vineyards of the most northerly of Piedmont's Nebbiolo-based wines. Carema is a long-lived wine that has acquired something of a cult following among Italian wine lovers. The local co-operative that is responsible for almost the entire production also runs a Bottega del Vino exclusively to exhibit its Carema wines.

From Carema, continue south on the SS26 to Ivrea, the home town of Olivetti, which has a 14th-century castle and a good museum. A few miles before Ivrea at Borgofranco d'Ivrea look for the centuries-old *balmetti*, over 130 cellar caves, still in use today.

Erbaluce di Caluso

South of Ivrea lies the town of Caluso and the zone of the curiously named white wine, Erbaluce di Caluso (loosely translated, green light of Caluso). Erbaluce is a traditional Piedmontese grape that has been rediscovered and found to be very suitable for the techniques of modern

A mediaeval watchtower stands guard over the vineyards of the Fiore company of Gattinara.

vinification. Unusually, it can be used for Spumante, for still wines and for a highly prized *passito* wine, made from dried grapes (see Glossary for explanation). The ancient name for this wine is *vin greco* (Greek wine): wine was introduced to Italy by the Greeks, and *greco* is a term generally used in Italy for bunches of grapes that grow in two clusters rather than one.

Caluso is west of the Dora Baltea river which passes through Ivrea. If at Ivrea the traveller turns off the SS26 and goes east of the river on the SS228, the next important stop is the castle of Roppolo on the banks of Lake Viverone.

The Enoteca Regionale della Serra in this castle is probably better known to the tourists who come to holiday by the lake than to Italians.

SPANNA
DEL PIEMONTE
RED WINE · PRODUCT OF ITALY

VINO DA TAVOLA

SELEZIONE
1983

750 ml   11,5% vol.

net contents 750 ml   1880   UMBERTO FIORE   alcohol 11,5% by vol.
Casa Vinicola in Gattinara

imbottigliato da – Produced and bottled by Umberto Fiore s.p.a · Gattinara · Italy

GATTINARA
DENOMINAZIONE DI ORIGINE CONTROLLATA

RED WINE · PRODUCT OF ITALY

SELEZIONE
1980

750 ml   12,5% vol.

net contents 750 ml   1880   UMBERTO FIORE   alcohol 12,5% by vol.
Casa Vinicola in Gattinara

imbottigliato da – Produced and bottled by Umberto Fiore s.p.a · Gattinara · Italy

Its history, though, is intimately connected with wine – and is reflected in the emblems on the coat of arms of one of its first lords. The story goes that one Caro Beccaria, servant to Lothario I, alerted his master to a poisoned chalice that he was just about to drink. Thankful for his escape, Lothario ennobled his servant, and gave him the castle of Roppolo and the right to display his own coat of arms, which is still in evidence at the castle today: three chalices full of red wine on a silver ground. Caro Beccaria then changed his name to Caro Bichiero (*bicchiere* meaning glass). Not all the history of this castle is quite so fortunate though; it is said to have the ghost of the knight Bernardo di Mazzei who was walled up alive in the castle in the 15th century.

The Enoteca specializes in the wines of the area around Vercelli and Novara: principally the Nebbiolo-based wines from around Gattinara, but Erbaluce from Caluso as well. It is also a hotel and restaurant and outdoor concerts are held here in the summertime.

Nearby the Lake of Viverone and the Museum La Steiva at Viverone itself are worth visiting.

Towards Milan

Taking the motorway E13 at Santhià and heading east, the traveller begins to encounter the rice fields that were originally planted to form a quickly floodable defence for Milan. Pasta as a food is a relatively recent addition to the northern Italian diet; risotto is more traditional here.

Fara to Gattinara

Exit on the SS299 at Agognate and the line of wine towns begins with Fara, then Sizzano, Ghemme and finally Gattinara. Lessona is a few miles to the east, Boca a few miles to the west. All of these towns give their names to Nebbiolo-based wines which have the potential to age well and are much lighter than their better-known southern Piedmontese cousins, Barolo and Barbaresco. The Nebbiolo in this area is called Spanna, and this is also the name used for wines that are not generally of the standard of those named after their towns of origin. Bramaterra is a similar wine but it is of noticeably better quality.

The spire of San Gaudenzio in Novara resembles Turin's more famous Mole Antonelliana.

CAREMA
Cantina dei Produttori Nebbiolo di Carema Via Nazionale 28. Tel: 0125 85256. All year, except July 15–Aug 15. T. E. Fr. TF. WS.

MAGGIORA
Cantine Antonio Vallana e Figlio snc Via Mazzini 3, Tel: 0322 87116. All year. t. E. Fr. G. TF. WS.

Gavi and Oltrepò Pavese

CASTEGGIO
Az. Agr. Boffalora Strada
Madonna 53. Tel: 0383
804557 (Luigi Poggi). May-
Sept. T. E. TF. WS.

CERTOSA DI PAVIA
Enoteca Lombarda
Via al Monumento 5. Tel:
0382 92393. Open March
19–Nov 1. Closed Mon. ER.
TP. WS. Restaurant.

GAVI
La Giustiniana Fraz.
Rovereto 5. Tel: 0143
682132. Fr. TF. WS.

**S. MARIA DELLA
VERSA**
Cantina Sociale
Via F. Crispi 15. Tel: 0385
79731. March-Oct, except
Aug. T. TP. WS.

In the border lands where
Lombardy, Emilia Romagna,
Piedmont and Liguria intersect there
are three distinct wine areas.

Gavi, Ovada and Acqui
South of Alessandria, east of the A26,
is the town of Gavi Ligure, which
shares its name with one of
Piedmont's finest grapes and Italy's
most prestigious white wines – Gavi.
The other white of the area, Cortese,
is more common, and can be found
all over the Alto Monferrato.

West of the A26 are the towns of
Ovada and Acqui Terme. Both have
a Dolcetto with their town names as
an *appellation*. Acqui Terme is also
well known for the sweet sparkling
dessert wine that has become

popular in North America, Brachetto
d'Acqui.

Since Roman times Acqui Terme
has been famous for its therapeutic
waters. Pliny the Elder was amused
by the contradictory name for the
local wines, '*vinum aquense*', or water
wines. However, the town coat of
arms is an aqueduct with a bunch of
grapes above it and Acqui is still
known both for its spring waters and
the wine.

Palazzo Robellini in the town is the
site of the Enoteca Regionale, which
specializes in the wines of this area.
Acqui is worth visiting anyway for
its cathedral, its castle and the
archaeological museum.

Colli Tortonesi
The hills of Tortona join the territory
of Piedmont to Lombardy. Tortona
itself has an interesting museum in a
15th-century palazzo but the wines
from the hills, Barbera and Cortese
dei Colli Tortonesi, lack much
beyond local appeal.

Oltrepò Pavese
Known as the Oltrepò Pavese
because it is literally on the other side
of the Po from Pavia, this is an area
that produces excellent sparkling
wines and a wide range of whites and
reds. The Bonarda is an especially
attractive red variety that produces a
somewhat softer wine than Barbera.

There is a *Strada del Vino* system to
follow in Oltrepò Pavese. But first it
is well worth a visit to the Enoteca
Lombarda at Certosa di Pavia, 7km
(4 miles) north of Pavia, to learn
about the wines. The Certosa
convent is a Renaissance masterpiece
and should not be missed. Pavia
itself has fine historic churches and
university buildings.

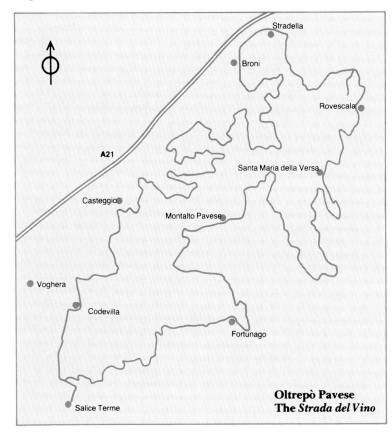

**Oltrepò Pavese
The *Strada del Vino***

Liguria

Liguria

For the foreigner Liguria has always meant holidays. English travellers have been attracted to the steeply sloping bays of the Italian Riviera for generations. Indeed, their old villas give the area a feeling of faded gentility even today.

It is for local consumption, and for the descendants of these travellers, who are now more likely to be making just a brief trip to Portofino, that wine is produced in Liguria. The peasant wine producer is a dying breed; working the steep slopes of the vineyards is difficult, and only a part-time activity for most of the vine-growers who remain.

Liguria's interest for the wine connoisseur lies in the tips at either end of its half-moon shape.

Soon after crossing the border from France near Ventimiglia, a left turn to the town of Dolceacqua brings one to the vineyards of Liguria's only serious red wine, the Rossese di Dolceacqua. Dolceacqua, with its ruined mediaeval castle and picturesque charm is typical of the villages of the Valle di Nervia.

At the other tip of the crescent is the delightful area of the Cinque Terre. Only the first of these five villages, Monterosso al Mare, is readily accessible by car. But to reach the others it is a pleasure to walk the cliff path through the olive groves and the vineyards of Liguria's most famous white wine, Cinque Terre. This dry wine goes well with the local fish, but the most prized version is the dessert wine, Schiacchetrá.

CAMPOROSSO
Viticoltori Biamonti
Località Giuncheo. Tel: 0184 28152 (Arnaldo Biamonti). All year. T. TP. WS.

DOLCEAQUA
Cantina del Rossese Crespi
Via Roma 33. Tel: 0184 36180. (Eraldo Crespi). All year. T. TP. WS.

GENOVA
Enoteca Sola Piazza Colombo 13r. Tel: 010 561329. 0830–1300, 1530–2000. Open all day Fri.
Ristorante 'Le Fate' which is also an Olioteca/Enoteca, specializes in authentic Ligurian regional cuisine. Via Ruspoli 31. Tel: 010 546401.

IMPERIA
Enoteca Fratelli Lupi Via Monti 13, Località Oneglia. Tel: 0183 21610. 0800–1245, 1600–2000. Closed Weds p.m. and Sun.

RIVAROLO
Museo Civico di Storia e Cultura Contadina Scuola Elementare Maria Boer, Salita al Garbo 47. Mon-Sat 0930–1330, 1400–1800, Sun 0930–1330. Country Life museum based on the lives of vine, olive and lavender growers.

Food and Festivals

FURTHER INFORMATION

Assessorato al Turismo
(Piedmontese Tourist
Board), Via Magenta 12,
10128 Torino. Tel: 011
57171.
**Associazione Consorzi
Vini D.O.C. Barolo,
Barbaresco e Vini d'Alba**
Piazza Savona 3, 12051
Alba. Tel: 0173 43202.
**Consorzio Vino D.O.C.
Asti Spumante** Piazza
Roma 10, 14100 Asti. Tel:
0141 54215.
**Consorzio Vini D.O.C.
Oltrepò Pavese** Piazza
San Francesco d'Assisi,
27043 Broni. Tel: 0385
51191.
**Regione Autonoma Valle
d'Aosta** Assessorato del
Turismo, Place Narbonne,
Aosta. Tel: 0165 303725.

FURTHER ADDRESSES

ALBA
Az. Vit. Ceretto srl Loc.
San Cassiano 34. Tel: 0173
42484 (Bruno Ceretto).
All year. T. E. TF. WS.
From 2–15 people.
Pio Cesare Via C. Balbo 6.
Tel: 0173 42407 (Pio and
Luciana Boffa). All year
except Aug and Christmas.
T. E. Fr. TF. WS.

BARBARESCO
**Produttori del
Barbaresco** Via Torino
52. Tel: 0173 635139
(Celestino Vacca). All year.
t. E. Fr. TF. WS.

BAROLO
G. Borgogno e Figli Via
Gioberti 1. Tel: 0173
56108. All year, office
hours, and Sat and Sun
a.m. t. E. Fr. G. TF. WS.
**Cantine Marchesi di
Barolo SpA** Via Alba 12.
Tel: 0173 56101. T. E. TF.

FOOD SPECIALITIES

Aosta
This is not an olive oil producing
region, but the butter and cheeses
are very good.
Cotoletta alla Valdostana: veal fried with
ham topped with fontina cheese.
Carbonade: meat stew with onions and
red wine.
Fonduta: Alpine fondue.

Liguria
Extra-virgin olive oil is the traditional
all-purpose condiment, fish the
traditional main course.
Pesto: ground mixture of basil, garlic,
oil and pine nuts, a sauce for pasta,
especially with *trenette* (pasta).
Torta Pasqualina: a savoury Easter
dish made of puff pastry filled with
ricotta and artichokes or spinach.
Fish: *baccalà* (salt cod), *bianchetti*,
(whitebait), *triglie* (red mullet).
Farinata: type of pizza bread made
with olive oil and chickpeas.

Piedmont
The produce of the *contadino* (peasant
farmer), such as maize, hazelnuts,
apples, rabbits, pigs and oxen
inspires the traditional dishes. In the
rice-growing area of Novara soups
and risottos are traditional. In the
Langhe truffles and mushrooms are
a speciality.
Bagna cauda: fresh vegetables
accompanied by a dip made with
olive oil, anchovies and much garlic.
Vitello tonnato: cold roast veal with a
creamy tuna fish sauce.
Brasato al Barolo: beef braised in
Barolo.
Finanziera: lights and brains in a wine
and cream sauce.
Fritto misto: mixed fried meats, brains
and semolina.
Bollito misto: mixed boiled meats.
Bonet: chocolate pudding.
Carne cruda all'Albese: thinly sliced raw
meat dressed with oil, lemon and
thin slices of parmesan.
Gianduja: hazelnut chocolates.

FESTIVALS

Aosta
January 30–31: AOSTA: St Orso fair -
handwoven textiles, wrought iron
and handcarved objects.
June 24: GRESSONEY: St John's Day –
procession in costume.
August: AOSTA: handicrafts fair.
August: LA THUILE: Fête des Bergers –
sports, folk events.

Liguria
June: GENOA: Palio of St Peter –
historical regatta
September: *Sagre dell'Uva* – wine
festivals in Cinque Terre, Vezzano
Ligure and Tivagna di Follo.

Piedmont
February: IVREA: carnival – events
recall death of mediaeval tyrant.
Battle of oranges.
March: ASTI: *Luna di Marzo* – annual
wine fair at traditional time for
bottling.
Easter: ALBA: annual Wine Festival.
May: ASTI: feast of Asti's patron saint,
San Secondo – folklore, cultural
events and sports. As a *finale*, the city
donates a banner to the church.
June: CALLIANO (Asti): Festa dell'
Agnolotto d'Asino – pasta filled with
donkey meat is offered to the public.
September: ASTI *Douja d'Or*: month-
long festival celebrating the local
wines. Some high quality wines on

show and a prestigious national competition.

September: ASTI: Palio of Asti – originating in 1275, horse race between various town districts. Parade in costume and flag throwing.

September: BAROLO (Cuneo): week-long festival of Barolo wine.

October (1st and 2nd Sundays): ALBA: national truffle fair, the *Fiera Nazionale del Tartufo*.

October: ALBA: tournament of the Hundred Towers and *Palio degli Asini* – recalling events in wars between Asti and Alba in the 13th century (besiegers from Asti staged a horse race around Alba's walls. The people of Alba retorted with a donkey race, as they had eaten all their horses). Truffle exhibition.

November: NIZZA MONFERRATO (Asti): food fair – cardoons (celery-like vegetable), truffles and wine.

**GHEMME
Antichi Vigneti di
Cantalupo sas** Via M. Buonarroti 5. Tel: 0163 840041 (Alberto Arlunno). All year. T. E. Fr. TF. WS.

Producers of the Co-operative Produttori del Barbaresco compare the wines. Together with Barolo, Barbaresco is one of Piedmont's most famous wines.

North Central Italy

Three distinct wine-producing areas make up north central Italy: the slopes and hills of the Adige and Isarca valleys which lead into Austria, the Valtellina that skirts the southern border with Switzerland, and the hills that are strung along the line between Bergamo and Lake Garda. Two regions of Italy are involved: Lombardy and Trentino-Alto Adige.

Lombardy is the industrial powerhouse of Italy, and alone is responsible for about 20 per cent of the gross national product. Milan is such a cosmopolitan city that it stands apart from the other widely differing principal cities of Bergamo, Brescia, Mantua and Pavia. Indeed, it is difficult to find a common characteristic for the Lombardi, a fact that is reflected in the wine production, too. Many excellent wines come from the hills above Bergamo, from Franciacorta west of Brescia, from the Valtellina, and from the hills of Lake Garda. But there is no great wine, no Barolo or Chianti, to seize the imagination.

Trentino-Alto Adige is a very divided area. In 1918 what was part of the Austro-Hungarian Tyrol was given to Italy, and renamed Alto Adige. Later Mussolini tried his best to Italianize the region by settling industrial workers from the South in the area, and incidentally promoting the wine of Santa Maddalena to the official rank of third-best wine in Italy (the other two were more obvious and sensible choices: Barolo and Barbaresco).

Alto Adige

The Alto Adige retained its independent spirit, however, and visitors are still constantly reminded by the inhabitants of where their real loyalties lie. German and Italian may be the dual official languages of the region, but German is more common.

In Alto Adige no less than 78 per cent of the wine produced is D.O.C., a high proportion for Italy, which in fact reflects the economic reality that it makes little sense in this area

of mountainous labour-intensive wine production to centralize the wines to make a mass product. Unfortunately, sometimes in the past it has been even better economic sense to plant apple orchards rather than vineyards.

Trentino

For its heritage, the Trentino prefers to look to Italy. Like Alto Adige, this is a mountainous region, with tourism as a major industry. But unlike Alto Adige, the Trentino is quite at home as part of the Italian state and, ironically, it has lost something of the sense of its own regional heritage.

In Trentino the proportion of D.O.C. wine is about 48 per cent, and 70 per cent of that is red. Both these figures are changing rapidly, however, as the popularity of Chardonnay grows and as both this wine and the excellent dry Trentino sparkling wines become elegible for the D.O.C.

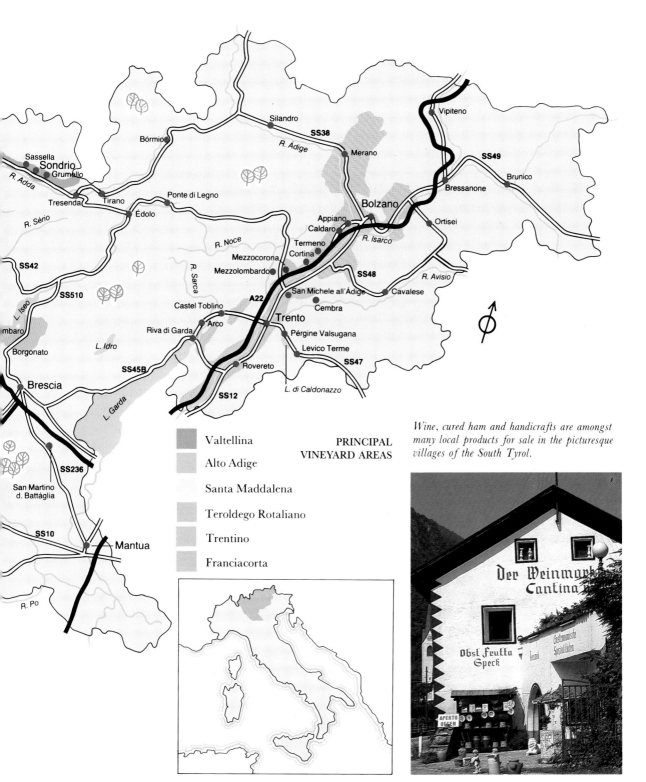

Sassella
Sondrio
Grumello
R. Adda
Bórmio
Silandro
SS38
R. Ádige
Merano
Vipiteno
SS49
Bressanone
Brunico
Tresenda
Tirano
Ponte di Legno
Édolo
Bolzano
Appiano
Caldaro
Ortisei
R. Sério
R. Noce
Termeno
Cortina
R. Isarco
SS42
R. Sarca
Mezzocorona
Mezzolombardo
SS48
R. Avisio
SS510
San Michele all'Ádige
Cavalese
L. Iseo
Castel Toblino
A22
Cembra
mbaro
Riva di Garda
Arco
Trento
L. Idro
Pérgine Valsugana
Borgonato
Levico Terme
SS47
SS45B
Rovereto
L. di Caldonazzo
SS12
Brescia
L. Garda
SS236
San Martino
d. Battáglia
SS10
Mantua
R. Po

PRINCIPAL
VINEYARD AREAS

Valtellina

Alto Adige

Santa Maddalena

Teroldego Rotaliano

Trentino

Franciacorta

Wine, cured ham and handicrafts are amongst many local products for sale in the picturesque villages of the South Tyrol.

South Tyrol – the Weinstrasse

Caldaro is typical of the picturesque towns along South Tyrol's Weinstrasse. Weinverkauf signs outside shops and wine producers' premises indicate that wine is for sale.

Wine production in what the Italians call Alto Adige and its German-speaking inhabitants call South Tyrol takes place in the Y-shaped area formed by the Adige and Iscaro river valleys branching off Bolzano.

The signposted *Weinstrasse* (wine road) is only one arm of the Y, but is a charming route among some of the prettiest villages in Italy.

Termeno is the first town of any size on this wine route and, as the

**South Tyrol
The *Weinstrasse***

town of origin for Gewürztraminer (Tramin is Termeno's German name) has a special fame in the wine world.

The visitor immediately becomes aware of the somewhat *gemütlich* charm of the area: the houses are often brown and white timbered traditional buildings decorated with geraniums. The men can still wear *lederhosen* without affectation. There are prominent signs for the sale of local wines. *Weinstube* is the Tyrolean equivalent of *osteria* (see page 50).

Lake Caldaro is surrounded by vineyards and dominated by a ruined castle on the opposite side to the town. Visit the museum of South Tyrolean Viticulture in the town of Caldaro.

Bolzano itself looks unpromising, but is worth visiting for the Gothic architecture of its churches as well as the Wine Fair held every spring.

APPIANO
Produzione e Commercio Vini Lindner Via Gravosa 29. Tel: 0471 52331. Weekdays (except Fri p.m.). t. G. TP. WS.
Società Co-operativa Viticoltori Alto Adige Via Circonvallazione 17. Tel: 0471 660060. Weekdays 0800–1230, 1400–1730. T (for weekends). G. TP. WS.

BOLZANO
Cantine Vini Lageder Via Druso 235. Tel: 0471 920164 (Alois Lageder). All year. T. E. G. TP. WS.

CALDARO
Casa Vinicola Kettmeir Via Cantina 4. Tel: 0471 963135 (Franco Kettmeir). T. E. G. TP. WS.
Museo del Vino Via Vicolo d'Oro. Tel: 0471 963168. Tues-Sat 0930–1200, 1400–1800, Sun 1400–1800. Closed Mon.

CORNAIANO
Cantina Produttori Colterènzio Weinstrasse 8, Tel: 0471 51246. All year except Sept and Oct. T. G. TP. WS. Min 10 visitors.

TERMENO
Az. Vin. Walch. Tel: 0471 860172 (Signor Rinner). Guided visits at 1715, June-Oct. E. G. Fr. TP. WS.
Cantina Vini Hofstätter Piazza Municipio 5. Tel: 0471 860161 (Paolo Foradori). Weekdays 0900–1200, 1430–1800. G. TP. WS.

Franciacorta

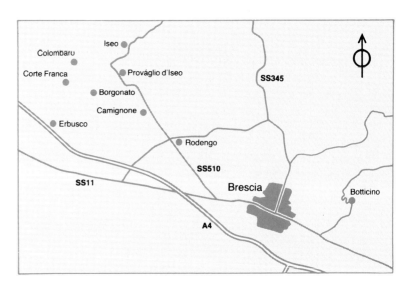

Of the wines of Lombardy, Lugana from the south of Lake Garda is an attractive, flowery and strong wine with a definite character. Other wines from the region are acceptable enough, but it is Franciacorta that combines the most attractive scenery with wines of real quality. All styles of wine are made here. Sparkling Franciacorta can be excellent and some of Italy's best *metodo champenois* wines come from this area.

Red Franciacorta is made from a unique mix of native Italian grapes, Nebbiolo and Barbera, and French grapes introduced in the last century, Cabernet and Merlot. Sadly, Franciacorta Rosso is drunk too young in response to the Italian craze for young wines; it is a delicious wine capable of great sophistication if allowed to age for a few years.

The Franciacorta wine route

No one is completely sure about the origin of the name Franciacorta; some say it comes from the time when French troops settled in the area in the 16th century; or perhaps from the time when tax exemption was granted to the local monasteries. Whatever lies in its name, this is an area of gentle hills full of the villas that were the country houses of the Lombard nobility.

From Brescia take the road to Iseo, stopping at Rodengo to see the abbey, and Provaglio d'Iseo to see the Romanesque church of San Pietro in Limosa. On the shores of Lake Iseo are olive and fruit trees mixed with vines, both benefiting from the temperate lakeside climate.

From Iseo take the road to the Corte Franca area. At Colombaro is the Villa Lana, home of one of the leading producers of Franciacorta wines, Giacomo Ragnoli; the villa gardens contain Italy's oldest Cedar of Lebanon. At Borgonato, Villa Berlucchi is synonymous with high quality Spumante.

A few kilometres further south is the notable wine centre of Erbusco; Maurizio Zanella of the Cà del Bosco company is famous for his Franciacorta Rosso and excellent sparkling *metodo champenois*. On the return to Brescia the Franciacorta vineyard-filled hills are to the north.

Valtellina

POGGIORIDENTI
Enoteca Regionale
1200–1600, 1900–2200.
Closed Tues. TP. ER.

Further addresses:
See also pp.46–47.

The town of Bórmio in the Valtellina. Well known as a skiing resort, it is also the home of a herbal digestif called Braulio. The onion-shaped dome of the church is an indication of Austro-Hungarian influence.

The 'powerful wines and terrible mountains' of the Valtellina were noted by Leonardo da Vinci in his travels. Both are much in evidence today. The dominant grape here is the same as for Barolo, the Nebbiolo, but it produces equally alcoholic, lighter-bodied wines, best in the *Superiore* version which is aged for at least two years, or the *Riserva* aged for four. An excellent heavier red is the Sfursat, a *passito* wine, made like Amarone from partially dried grapes (see Glossary).

The wine route from Como
From the northern tip of Lake Como the main road to Sondrio (SS38) crosses the Adda after Morbengo, and the regular pattern of stone-terraced vineyards soon becomes apparent. Vineyards are on both sides of the Adda up to a height of 1200 metres but the best are those on the northern bank of the river; they get more sun. The mountains shelter both banks from violent extremes of temperature.

Valtellina's sub-regions
Just before Sondrio is the first of the four Valtellina Superiore sub-regions, Sassella. Visit the 15th-century church of Madonna della Sassella surrounded by vineyards. The wine, like all Valtellina Superiore wines, is best after three to five years' ageing, and goes well with roasts and strong cheeses.

After the provincial capital, Sondrio, is the sub-region of Grumello, whose wine is said to have a slight almond taste from the traditional secondary blending grape, the Brugnola. Visit the Enoteca Regionale at Poggioridenti for a full tasting of Valtellina wines at the Enoteca's *osteria*, called the Crotto after the traditional Valtelline cellars excavated in the rock.

Next along the main road is the sub-region of Inferno, so called because the hill terraces become so hot in the summer. The wine is very long-lived and takes longer to become ready for drinking than its lighter cousins.

Tresenda marks the limit of the sub-region of Valgella wine, almost all of which is exported to the traditional market for Valtellina wines in general, Switzerland.

Trentino

Trentino is almost entirely mountainous, and vine-growing is restricted to the valley floors and hillsides, mainly along the Adige, Cembra and Sarca rivers.

Trento, the scene of the famous Council of Trent (1545–63), is a good starting point for your tour. Visit the former palace of the Prince-Bishops at the Castello del Buonconsiglio, and the Duomo.

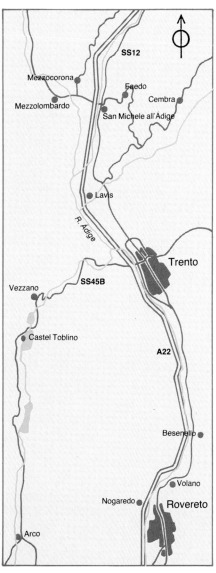

Principal wines

Dry sparkling wines are a speciality of the Trentino wineries. The best of Italian *metodo champenois* wines, Ferrari, is made here.

Chardonnay is the up and coming white, but made in the fresh Italian fashion rather than aged in oak. Other whites to look out for are Pinot Bianco and Pinot Grigio, Riesling and Traminer. A curiosity is the Vino Santo produced only in the Sarca valley from Nosiola grapes dried on racks and pressed about Eastertime.

Teroldego and Marzemino are the most famous Trentino reds. Caldaro, Lagrein and Casteller are lighter reds. The Cabernet is particularly drinkable.

The wine routes: Cembra and Teroldego

From Trento go north to Lavis on the SS12. At Lavis turn east to Cembra for a pretty route up the valley whose steep right bank is covered with terraces of vines. Cembra's co-operative, its Cantina Sociale, is the highest in Europe, and specializes in Caldaro and Müller-Thurgau.

Descending the valley again and taking the road to San Michele all'Adige via Faedo, the vines are trained in the centuries-old *pergola trentina* fashion that is unique to Trentino.

San Michele has the well-known Istituto Agrario Provinciale and Experimental Wine School in the buildings of an old monastery, where wines may be tasted. The folk museum here is also worth a visit.

Crossing to the other bank of the Adige brings one to the plains of Mezzocorona and Mezzolombardo.

NOGAREDO TRENTO
Az. Agr. Letrari
Palazzo Lodron. Tel: 0464 432568 (Signor Letrari). t. All year. E. G. TF. WS. 16th-century cellars.

TRENTO
Enoteca Lunelli
Largo Carducci 12. 0900–1200, 1500–1900. Closed Sun, and Mon a.m.
Ferrari Fratelli Lunelli SpA Via del Ponte della Ravina 15, 38040 Trento. Tel: 0461 922500 (Dr A. Michela). All year except Aug, Nov and Dec. T. E. TP. WS. Minimum 10 visitors.

These are the towns of an excellent red suitable for ageing, the *principe di Trentino*, Teroldego.

Return to Trento via the hills and light red wines of Sorni.

Casteller and Marzemino

Wherever you go in Trentino, fortresses and vineyards line the route. From Trento south towards Rovereto, there is a spectacular mediaeval castle at Besenello.

Marzemino, the red wine celebrated in Mozart's opera *Don Giovanni*, comes from Isera and the valley of Vallagarina. Further south, Avio is well known for the quality of its Casteller wine, a light red made from Lambrusco, Merlot and Schiava, taking its name from the Casteller hill just to the south of Trento at Mattarello.

The Sarca valley

A steep mountain road west from Trento leads to this attractive valley, also known as the valley of the lakes.

Castel Toblino is a romantic lakeside castle surrounded by vineyards, and further down the valley in Arco there is an ancient palazzo. Tourist wine stalls, *punti di vendita*, increase in frequency nearer to Lake Garda.

**ROVERETO
Az. Agr. Conti Bossi
Fedrigotti** Via Unione 43. Tel: 0464 439250. All year except last two weeks Sept and Oct. T. E. G. Fr. TP. WS.

Vineyards in the hills of Trentino blaze gold in autumn.

Food and Festivals

FURTHER INFORMATION
Assessorato Provinciale per l'Agricoltura e le Foreste Via Brennero 6, 39100 Bolzano. Tel: 0471 992111. *South Tyrol Wine Guide* and *South Tyrol Wine Companion* by Tom O'Toole are available here (or from Camera di Commercio I.A.A., Via Garibaldi 4, 39100 Bolzano).
Azienda Provinciale Turismo Trentino Corso III Novembre 132, 38100 Trento. Tel: 0461 980000.
Comitato Vitivinicolo Trentino Piazza A. Vittoria 3, 38100 Trento. Tel: 0461 987094.
Consorzio Vini D.O.C. Bresciani Via Vittorio Emanuel II, 61, 25100 Brescia. Tel: 030 45061.
Consorzio Vini D.O.C. Valtellina Centro Foianini, Via Valeriana, 23100 Sondrio. Tel: 0342 216433.

LOMBARDY

COMO
Enoteca Museo S. Silvestro Via Manzoni 16. Tel: 031 269317. Weekdays 0900–1200, 1400–1830. Closed Sat p.m. and Sun. Folk museum and wine shop.

MILAN
Enoteche (specialist wine shops):
Luigi Cotti Via Solferino 42.
Maria Luisa Ronchi Via S. Maurilio 7.
N'Ombra de Vin Via S. Marco 2.
Solci Via Morosini 19.
Vino Vino Via Speronari 4 and Via S. Gottardo 13 and Viale Pasubio 6/8.

FOOD SPECIALITIES

Torggelen in the Alto Adige
Torggelen is a dialect word that came from the mediaeval word for the place where wine was served, and before that, from the Latin *torculum* meaning wine press.

Today, *torggelen* describes the very pleasant habit of late autumn trips into the countryside, where the colours of autumn trees and the last of the sun's warmth can be enjoyed at an outdoor table at the same time as the first of the new season's wine is ready. Roast chestnuts, home-made sausage with *sauerkraut* and *speck* (mountain-cured ham) are the normal accompaniments, served in the characteristic hillside *trattorie* or *weinstuben*.

Local cuisine
In the past Trentino and Alto Adige had similar cooking traditions based on shared Hapsburg and Slavonic influences. Now the Trentino has become more typically Italian

regional, whereas Alto Adige has been at pains to preserve its own particular traditions. Trentino cooking does exist, but only in the home; it is not a restaurant culture.

Some dishes are common to the two regions. Soups are encountered more frequently than pasta, for example *Canederli trentini* (*knodel tirolesi* in Alto Adige), a broth with gnocchi of liver.

Lombard dishes
Lombardy has given us some of the better-known Italian dishes: *Risotto alla milanese* – risotto with saffron; *Cotoletta milanese* – similar to *Wienerschnitzel*; *Ossobuco*; and *panettone* – the traditional Christmas cake.

Foods from Brescia
Naturally, the best food of Lakes Iseo and Garda is the fish from the lakes and the olive oil from the lakeside.

Rovato is noted for its meat. The plains of Brescia are a great source of cheese and butter. Some of the more noted cheeses are: *Grana Padano*,

FESTIVALS

Alto Adige
End May: BOLZANO: festival of the *Schutzen*, folk festival based around parade of mediaeval militia.
Spring: BOLZANO: Bolzano Wine Fair (*Bozner Weinkost*) in the halls of the Laurin Hotel – a presentation of the recent vintage to the trade and to connoisseurs.
August: RIVA DEL GARDA (Trento): National Italian Folklore Festival.
Mid-August: VALDAORA: wine-tasting week.
End September: TERMENO:

International Tasting of Traminer Aromatico/ Gewürztraminer at Traminer – tasting of international wines of this grape.
Mid-October: ORA: Unterland wine tasting week.
October: MERANO: *Festa dell'Uva*.

Trentino
February: NAGO-TORBOLE: carnival festival of spaghetti, fish from the lake and tasting of wines from the Valle del Sarca.
February: RIVA DEL GARDA (Località Varone): carnival festival of *polenta* and sausage with local wines.

similar to parmesan, but not so expensive; *Gorgonzola*; and *Taleggio*, a semi-soft cheese from the town of the same name.

Specific dishes include: *Risotto alla pitocca* – chicken risotto; *Minestra mariconda* – pasta in broth; *Tinca all'Iseana* – beef roast in oil, butter and laurel, coated with breadcrumb, cheese, rosemary and parsley.

Valtellina meats and cheeses
The most famous product of the Valtellina is an international favourite: *bresaola*, the cured and dried beef. There is a version made from raw goat's meat, *violino*, so called because of the traditional method of carving it in a way that recalls the playing of a violin.

In the province of Sondrio as a whole, specialities include: cheeses such as *Bitto, Formaggelle* and *Stracchino*; dishes based on mushrooms; and the inevitable corn dish, *polenta*, a staple of northern Italy, and particularly of Lombardy and the Veneto.

Mid March: TRENTO: Fair of St Joseph. Flower festival.
April/May: TRENTO: regional exhibition of wines from throughout Trentino, together with Grappa and sparkling wines.
August: FIERA DI PRIMIERO: festival of wines and fruit.
August: RIVA DEL GARDA: National Italian Folklore Festival.
August: PERGINE VALSUGANA: festival of wines from the Trentino.
August/September: PADERGNONE: exhibition and sale of local products – wine, fruit, Grappa and crafts.
September: ARCO: important festival of

sparkling wines from the Trentino with tastings and sales of wine.
September: CALDONAZZO: sausage and *polenta* festival with tastings of local wine.
September: ROVERETO: exhibition of wines of the Vallagarina.
September: TRENTO: exhibition of Grappa.
October: TRENTO: exhibition of *metodo classico* (Champagne method) sparkling wines of Trentino.

Lombardy
Lake Garda is a tourist centre with exhibitions and festivals throughout the season. (Local producers of olive oil claim health-giving properties for their oil because of the lakeside climate.) Salò, site of the puppet Italian state set up by Hitler after the collapse of Mussolini in 1943, has an important musical festival every summer; Gardone, Desenzano and Sirmione often have exhibitions or concerts. Polpenazze has a wine festival, Limone has a festival of fish from Lake Garda.

Specific festivals include:
Epiphany: PREMANA (Como): costume procession of the Three Kings.
February: BAGOLINO (Brescia): carnival procession with costumed groups of opposing revellers.
February: VALTORIA (Bergamo): carnival procession.
End May: LEGNANO (Milan): *Sagra del Carroccio* and *Palio delle Contrade* – historical pageant recalling victory of Lombard League over Frederick Barbarossa in 1176.
Beginning June: MILAN: festival of the *navigli* (canals); folk festival.
October: COMO: music festival.
End Nov: GORGONZOLA: festival of ground corn, *polenta*, and *Gorgonzola* cheese.

VALTELLINA

CHIURO
Casa Vinicola Aldo Rainoldi
Via Stelvio 128. Tel: 0342 482225 (Giuseppe Rainoldi). Closed Aug. t. E. Fr. TF. WS.
Nino Negri Via Ghibellini 3. Tel: 0342 482521 (Casimiro Maule). All year. T. E. G. TF. WS.

SONDRIO
Enologica Valtellinese SpA Via Piazzi 29. Tel: 0342 212047 (Alberto Pacchi). All year 1000–1200, 1500–1800. Closed weekends. t. E. TF. WS. Minimum 8 visitors.

TRENTINO

MEZZOCORONA
Cantine Mezzacorona Via IV Novembre 13. Tel: 0461 605163 (Andreas Kossler). All year. T. E. G. Fr. TF. WS.

MEZZOLOMBARDO
Equipe Trentina Spumanti srl Piazza San Giovanni 32a, Mezzolombardo. Tel: 0464 432568 / 0461 601512 (Signor Letrari). All year except Aug. T. G. TF. WS.

ROVERE DELLA LUNA
Az. Vin. Gaierhof Via IV Novembre. Tel: 0461 658514. All year, except Aug. T. E. G. Fr. TF. WS.

VOLANO
Lagariavini SpA Via Nazionale. Tel: 0464 411000 (Sara Schwarz). All year 0830–1200, 1400–1700. T. E. G. TP. WS.

The Veneto

O nce the site of fierce fighting in the Risorgimento and World War I, the Veneto is a peaceful region, and its plains and foothills, decorated by villas and cypresses, are redolent of prosperity. Many towns proclaim peace on their statues of the Lion of Saint Mark: *Pax Tibi Marce Evangelista Meus.*

Set within the natural boundaries of the Dolomites in the north, the Venetian lagoon in the east, and Lake Garda in the west, it is easy to see why the Veneto has always been popular with the tourist. Its cities are rich in art and culture. Verona is famous for the opera festival held every year in its Roman amphitheatre, and for the Romanesque church of San Zeno with its marvellous mediaeval bronze doors; Vicenza is the city of the great Renaissance architect Palladio (1501–80); Padua has the basilica of S. Antonio, and Giotto's masterly fresco series in the Scrovegni Chapel; and Venice, of course, is unique.

The Lion of St Mark in Venice is both the symbol of the Evangelist and of the power of Venice's trading empire. Similar statues can still be found in towns throughout the old Venetian territories.

While the Veneto does not produce anything like the volume of wine that comes from the southern regions of Italy, its wines are the most widely available of all Italian wines abroad. Soave, Valpolicella and Bardolino are instantly recognizable names. Unfortunately, in the recent past the more commercial producers of Verona were quick to flood the

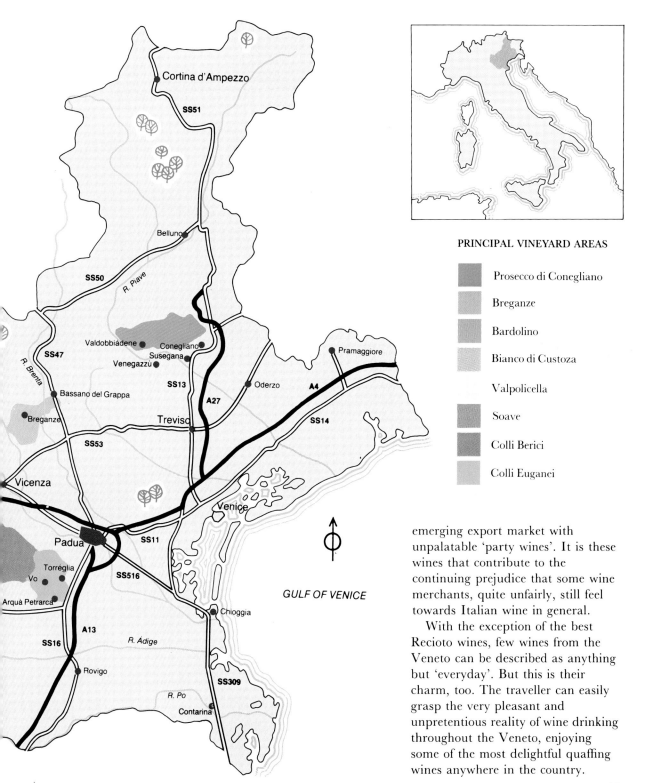

PRINCIPAL VINEYARD AREAS

Prosecco di Conegliano

Breganze

Bardolino

Bianco di Custoza

Valpolicella

Soave

Colli Berici

Colli Euganei

GULF OF VENICE

emerging export market with unpalatable 'party wines'. It is these wines that contribute to the continuing prejudice that some wine merchants, quite unfairly, still feel towards Italian wine in general.

With the exception of the best Recioto wines, few wines from the Veneto can be described as anything but 'everyday'. But this is their charm, too. The traveller can easily grasp the very pleasant and unpretentious reality of wine drinking throughout the Veneto, enjoying some of the most delightful quaffing wines anywhere in the country.

49

Verona and Vicinity

The mediaeval castle of Soave has a grand total of 24 towers.

GAMBELLARA
Cantine Zonin SpA Via Borgolecco 9. Tel: 0444 444031 (Dr F. Zuffellato, Signor Zaratin). All year except Aug. E. T. TF. WS.

MONFORTE D'ALPONE
Anselmi SpA Via S. Carlo 46. Tel: 045 7611488 (Lorella Bonomi). T. E. Fr. WS (no tasting).

SOAVE
Enoteca del Soave Via Roma 19. Tel: 045 7681588. Daily 0900–1300, 1500–2400. Closed Wed. EP. TP. WS. Snacks.

TORREGLIA
Girolamo Luxardo SpA Via Romana 36. Tel: 049 5211 (Franco Luxardo, Rosy Atzei). All year except Aug and fortnight after Christmas. E. G. Fr. TF. WS. Liqueur specialist.

Verona is a charming city, particularly rich in Roman remains, Gothic churches and Renaissance palaces. Despite the almost uninterrupted occupation by tourists all year round, its people are invariably courteous. Because of the excellent motorway connections with the North, their second language tends to be German rather than English.

Verona is also the site of the most important wine fair in the Italian calendar, VINITALY. This takes place every April and is a serious event intended above all for the trade. It is where the Italian producers meet to taste each other's wines, exchange the latest gossip, and, most important of all, to establish new contacts with foreign and Italian buyers. But it is also possible to pay to enter the fair at certain times in the week as a member of the public. Indeed, it is remarkable to see the patient lengths to which an Italian producer will go,

if he has no potential trade client waiting, to educate a member of the public about his wines. All the best wines are on display and it is an unparalleled opportunity for the connoisseur.

Trattorie **and** *osterie*
Verona is rich in restaurants and *trattorie*, but particularly useful for the wine traveller, who cannot be guaranteed a good selection of wines in a lower level restaurant or trattoria, is the survival of the *osteria* in Verona. These are traditional wine bars where it is possible to drink wines by the glass and, usually, to have a snack as well. They vary from the dingy local haunt serving indifferent wine, to the wine bar that serves good quality wines and local foods to go with them. There are 27 *osterie* in Verona; the Bottega dei Vini is most popular, and always full at the time of VINITALY. For tasting only, the Cantina dal Zovo is interesting and central.

Soave
From Verona, take the main road to Vicenza (SS11) for about 20km (12 miles) to the famous wine town of Soave.

In Via Roma there is an Enoteca at which one can taste and buy wine. It is also possible to arrange visits to the local Cantina Sociale, one of the largest and most advanced in Italy.

Soave as a wine has been much maligned. While there is no doubt that a great sea of indifferent wine is still produced, new techniques of vinification and the creation of single-vineyard Soaves have done much to redeem this wine. The best Soave can be as good as white burgundy and have as much depth of flavour.

Colli Berici and Euganei

East of Verona there are two other areas of wine interest: the hills south of Vicenza called the Colli Berici, and the hills south-west of Padua, the Colli Euganei. Each area produces seven D.O.C. wines, mainly from foreign grape varieties such as Cabernet and Merlot that were brought into the area about a century ago, but also from varieties such as Tocai and Pinot Bianco.

The Colli Berici are famous for their aristocratic villas built by the patrician inhabitants of Vicenza, though the Palladian villas of the area are mostly spread around the southern limits of the hills and just outside Vicenza to the north.

The Colli Euganei produce a curiosity in the highly perfumed Moscato Fior d'Arancio, which is said to have been the cause of Petrarch's conversion to wine in 1370 when he arrived at the town named Arquà Petrarca in his honour.

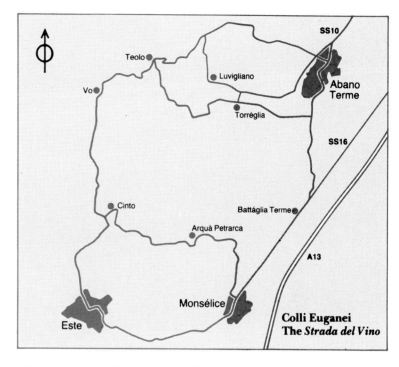

The Roman arena of Verona is part of the rich historic legacy of a city that is home to the wine fair VINITALY. Verona is also the chief city of the region that produces Bardolino, Soave and Valpolicella.

VERONA
Fratelli Bolla SpA Piazza Citadella 3. Tel: 045 594055 (Giuseppe Butti). Jan-July, Sept-Nov. T. E. G. TF. WS. Minimum 5 visitors.
Istituto Enologico Italiano SpA Piazzetta Chiavica 2. Tel: 045 590366. All year. E. G. WS.
Fratelli Pasqua SpA P.O. Box 448, Via Belviglieri 30. Tel: 045 522300 (Carlo Pasqua). T. E. Fr. G. TF. WS.

VINITALY Annual Fair Verona Fair Halls. Tel: 045 588111. Mid April. Public admission 1400–1900. Entry charge. TF.

VO EUGANEO
Enoteca Az. Vin. Villa Sceriman Via dei Colli 68. Tel: 049 9940123 (Sara Soranzo). All year 1000–1200, 1500–2000. Closed Mon. t. TF. WS.

The Wine Roads – Bardolino

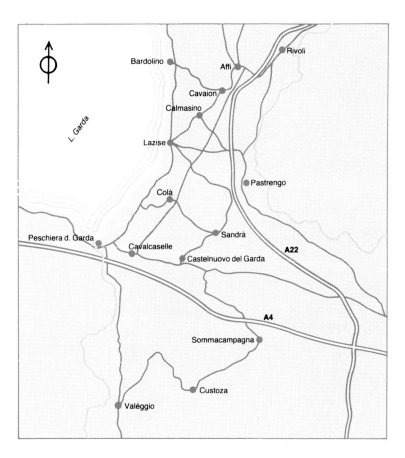

are intermittent. However, with the aid of a detailed local map you can make a very pleasant excursion to the towns of Bardolino production on the eastern shores of Lake Garda, and to the hills between the lake and the Adige river.

Verona to Lake Garda

From Verona take the main road to Lake Garda and the town of Peschiera del Garda, an important Austrian stronghold in the years before the great national uprising, the Risorgimento. There are remains of the 19th-century fort.

Visit the Arvedi d'Emilei company at Cavalcaselle, on the way to Peschiera. The present count and his son take an active interest in wine producing on the estate: the cellars are in their historic country villa.

To the south lies Bianco di Custoza land, to the north, after a small overlap with Bianco di Custoza, is the territory of Bardolino.

Along the coast road there are numerous *punto di vendita* signs, and also the signs for the olive oil routes around Lake Garda. There is an olive oil museum just before Cisano, and the local oil is reputed to be particularly good since the microclimate of Lake Garda does not permit the survival of the parasites on the olive fruit.

The town of Lazise retains its characteristic crenellations, dating from the time when it was the Venetian Republic's main outlet onto Lake Garda. It has an Enoteca in Via Porta del Lion.

Bardolino

Bardolino itself is a small tourist-orientated town of some charm; but in season it is totally impossible to

BARDOLINO
Villa Guerrieri Rizzardi
Az. Agr. dei Conti Guerrieri Rizzardi, Piazza Principe Amedeo 1. Tel: 045 7210028. Open Apr-Oct. T. E. G. TP. WS. Small wine museum. (See also p.55.)

CALMASINO DI BARDOLINO Az. Agr. Colli dei Cipressi Via Tre Contrè 1. Tel: 045 7235078. Weekdays 0900–1200, 1400–1800. T. WS. TF.

Bardolino is a very ancient wine, but not a pretentious one; it is a light, fruity red with a characteristic cherry-stone taste. Normally a bright garnet colour, it is also made in the rosé Chiaretto version that is a perfect summer day's picnic wine, well adapted to the sybaritic lifestyle of those who holiday on Lake Garda.

In theory there is an established itinerary to follow to discover the wines of Bardolino, with a route indicated by *Strada del Vino* signposts, and producers who are willing to sell to the public – advertising the fact with their *punto di vendita* signs.

In practice there are indeed quite a number of *punti di vendita* or direct sale (*vendita diretta*) signs, but unfortunately the directional signs park nearby and the streets themselves are too narrow to admit traffic anyway. Do not miss the 11th-century frescoed church of San Severo just by the main road out of Bardolino to Garda.

All of the town's grocery shops and a couple of specialist wineshops sell Bardolino wine, especially that of the most important producer, Azienda Agricola Guerrieri Rizzardi. Countess Rizzardi's villa takes up the southern flank wall of the town and a doorway in this wall leads to the villa's own small museum of wine-making implements, and its wineshop. All the Guerrieri Rizzardi wines are estate bottled and the Countess is a proponent of organic cultivation for the vineyards and non-pasteurization for the wines. She has recently introduced single-vineyard versions of all her wines and the quality is consistently high.

The hills of Bardolino

From Bardolino the *Strada del Vino* leads the traveller to Affi, Cavaion, Calmasino, Pastrengo, Sandrà, Colà, Castelnuovo del Garda, and back to Peschiera. These small villages in the range of hills between Lake Garda and the Adige valley are the heartland of Bardolino and have numerous *punti di vendita* for both wine and olive oil. An interesting diversion is from Affi to Rivoli Veronese, the site of a Napoleonic victory in 1797 and a subsequent monument and museum. The castle just outside the village looks down the valley of the Adige, the invasion route from the north.

The wine town of Bardolino has a maze of narrow streets. The town is pleasantly placed on the shores of Lake Garda: its delicatessens are well stocked with local wines.

12% Alcohol by volume

Vigneto   Vigneto   Il Tiler

Arsere

Tacheto

Strada di Tacheto

Arsere   Vigneto   San Pietro in Cariano

sassi

TACCHETTO

Bardolino
denominazione di origine controllata
classico
imbottigliato all'origine dal viticoltore
GUERRIERI RIZZARDI · VERONA · ITALIA

750 ml e

Product of Italy   ESTATE BOTTLED   Dry red wine

CAVALCASELLE
Az. Agr. Arvedi d'Emilei
Via Palazzo Emilei 5. Tel: 045 7553662 (Pietro Arvedi d'Emilei). All year. T. G. TF. WS. Cantina in historic villa.

COLA DI LAZISE
Az. Agr. Le Tende
Loc. Le Tende. Tel: 045 7570121 (Mauro Fortuna). t. E. G. TF. WS. Maximum 20 visitors.

PASTRENGO
Lamberti Loc. Bagnol. Tel: 045 7170043 (Signor Liut). All year except Aug. T. E. G. TF. WS.

The Wine Roads – Valpolicella

The Masi winery, one of the top producers of Valpolicella, is set in gently rolling countryside, surrounded by vineyards and cherry trees.

Valpolicella is produced on the north bank of the Adige in the foothills of the Lessini mountains. The area to the west of Verona from Pedemonte to S. Ambrógio is the Classico area, but the Valpolicella of the Pantena valley is generally better suited to ageing.

Valpolicella can be a delight, full of fragrance and flavour. It can also be a watery travesty of a wine. Apart from the enormous difference between the top quality producers such as Quintarelli, Allegrini, Bertani, Tedeschi, and Masi, and the industrial concerns who sell what is almost a cooking wine, the secret of a rich and flavoursome Valpolicella lies in the vinification. Wines made by the *ripasso* method, which involves fermentation on the lees, have an extra richness.

Valpolicella, like Soave and Gambellara, can also be made in the Recioto form, which involves selecting grapes from the outside top edges of the bunch; the grapes are then left to dry on racks, concentrating in sugar prior to fermentation in the New Year. Recioto can be a sweet dessert wine, a sparkling wine, or it can create a rich, dry wine, the famous Recioto Amarone di Valpolicella.

Valpantena

You can make an interesting excursion that combines the pleasure of wine travelling with the sight of magnificent mountain scenery by driving up the Valpantena from Verona and then descending into the Valpolicella.

From Verona take the road to Grezzana, due north of the city. The Cantina Sociale of Valpantena has signs of the Consorzio for Valpolicella indicating the zone of production. The bishop in their logo is San Zeno, a lover of this wine.

Just before Grezzana on the left of the road is the imposing Palladian Villa Arvedi, often used for official wine presentations. This area is where Bertani's Valpolicella Valpantena, a long-lived version of this famous wine, is produced.

Valpolicella

By winding up past the marble quarries of the Valpantena eventually one emerges into mountain landscape. At Fosse the descent begins into the Progno valley and the Valpolicella, whose territory is indicated by vineyards and cherry trees (which have the added function of binding the earth of the vineyard terraces with their roots).

From the attractive town of Fumane, take another winding road to Marano, up through the mixed olive tree and vine plantations. There are several *punto di vendita* signs from now on, but *vino contadino*

(home-made wine) can be a trap: it's rarely good quality unless, as happens, the *contadino* has bought his wine from the local co-operative.

At the end of the valley in San Floriano there is a regional office of the Valpolicella Consorzio; Villa Lebrecht is an Enoteca and the site of experimental vineyards.

Here one can either turn left to Pedemonte, glimpsing the rustic Palladian Villa Serego (not open to the public), now the headquarters of the Santa Sofia wine company, or right to S. Ambrógio, an important centre for Classico wines. At Pedemonte turn north to Negrar, where you can buy wine at the Cantina Sociale. On the opposite side of the stream that runs through the town you can visit the other villa of the Rizzardi family, with its famous 18th-century gardens and a *punto di vendita* (wine-tasting room) in the courtyard – not to be missed.

NEGRAR DI VALPOLICELLA
Cantina Sociale di Valpolicella Tel: 045 7500070. All year except Aug. Closed Sat and Mon. T. TF. WS.
Vignaiolo Quintarelli Via Cerè 1. Tel: 045 7500016 (Giuseppe Quintarelli). T. WS. TF.
Villa Rizzardi Poiega Az. Agr. dei Conti Guerrieri Rizzardi. (Office: Piazza Amedeo 1, Bardolino.) Tel: 045 7210028. Open Apr-Oct. T. E. G. TP. WS. Famous 18th-century garden. Booking not necessary for wine sale in villa courtyard. (See also pp.52–53.)

S. AMBROGIO DI VALPOLICELLA
Masi Agricola SpA Loc. Gargagnago. Tel: 045 7701696 (Sandro Boscaini). All year except mid-Aug. E. G. Fr. TF. WS. Visit also to Serego Alighieri estate (wine distributed by Masi, villa owned by descendant of Dante).

For further addresses, see p.62

The Wine Roads – Custoza

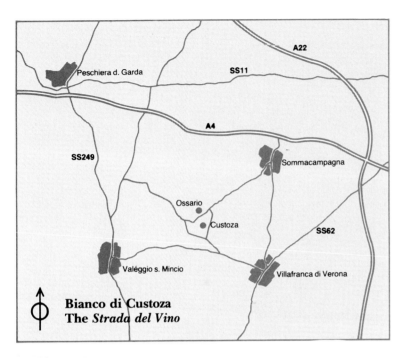

Bianco di Custoza
The *Strada del Vino*

PESCHIERA DEL GARDA
Az. Vin. Zenato snc
Via S. Benedetto 8, S.
Benedetto di Lugana. Tel:
045 7550300 (Anna Zenato,
Rosaria Battaglia). All
year. T. E. G. Fr. TF. WS.
Maximum 10 visitors.

SIRMIONE
Enoteca del Lugana
Viale Marconi 40/42. Tel:
030 916465. 1000–1230,
1500–1900. Closed Wed.
EP. TP. WS.

SOMMACAMPAGNA
**Az. Agr. Le Vigne di San
Pietro**. Tel: 045 510016
(Carlo Nerozzi). All year. t.
E. TF. WS.

Bianco di Custoza takes its name
from the historic town of Custoza
about 18km (11 miles) south-west of
Verona. As a wine it is enjoying
considerable success because it is an
alternative to Soave, but is not
tainted with the downmarket image
that Soave has acquired through
over-production and commercial
exploitation. At its best this is a
light, fragrant and fruity white wine
to be drunk within 18 months or so
of production. As with the whole area
around Lake Garda, viticulture has
ancient traditions here, and provably
early origins. Documentary evidence
traces wine production here back to
the 1st century AD.

Of all the wine roads near Verona,
these are the most clearly marked,
an unusual pleasure. It is easy to
follow the main *Strada del Vino* with
its *punto di vendita* signs, and there are
several large roadside hoardings
which advertise the route and its
points of interest.

Bianco di Custoza wine route
The starting point for the traveller
from Verona is a turning off the
motorway about 10km (6 miles) west
of Verona, to the town of
Sommacampagna. Here one picks up
signs for the *Strada del Vino* and finds
several *punti di vendita*.

Sommacampagna itself is a noted
centre for wine production; records
referring to the mediaeval town of
Summacampania (it is more like a
village today), prove that vineyards
flourished here in AD 938.

Just outside Sommacampagna on
the way to Custoza there is a large
sign or hoarding showing the wine
route, which may be useful for
planning the rest of the trip.

Before you reach Custoza there is
a Cantina Sociale with its customary
punto di vendita.

Custoza
This is a small town on two hills,
each dominated by a particular

building. On the highest hill is the Ossario di Custoza, a monument and an ossarium (literally a bone house, or burial vault) for the Austrian and Italian dead of the Risorgimento. The slopes nearby were the sites of their battles.

The monument is an imposing needle-shaped structure built at the end of the 19th century. It is open to the public and, on a fine day, gives a wonderful vantage point over the immense plain of the Mincio river and hills around the south of Lake Garda. You can see the hillsides of Bianco di Custoza production lying in a semicircle to the north of the town.

The other hill of Custoza is topped by the Villa Pignatti Morano, a grand building restored in the 1930s but retaining the original pockmarks of 19th-century battles in its walls.

Villafranca and Valéggio

Once past the hilltop villa, the *Strada del Vino* forks, left to Villafranca, right to Valéggio sul Mincio. On the way down the hill to Villafranca there is a *punto di vendita* with demijohns of wine displayed outside. This is an attractively wooded area with winding country roads.

Valéggio is dominated by a hilltop mediaeval castle and has a botanical park in the grounds of the Villa Segurtà. From Valéggio the *Strada del Vino* goes to Peschiera del Garda, where the Bianco di Custoza zone overlaps with Bardolino.

Villa Pignatti Morano is the first sight of Custoza for the traveller approaching from Villafranca.

Treviso – the Red Wine Roads

Treviso is characterized by numerous canals and houses constructed over water, just as if the builders had come from a few kilometres further south to copy Venice on a more human scale. Much of the layout of this city dates from early mediaeval times when it was an important cultural centre. Indeed, the most important wine co-operative of the area, the Marca Trevigiana (Marches of Treviso), recalls this era in its name and logo of fairytale castle towers.

Strada del Vino Rosso: the wines

This road covers the area between Treviso and Conegliano in a semi-circular route via Oderzo. It winds its way across the plain of the Piave, the source of some excellent reds, and a few good whites, too. The reds would be better still if they were allowed to age a little longer, but the fashion at the moment is to drink them young and fresh.

As is normal in north-east Italy the vineyards are planted with a mixture of indigenous vines, such as Verduzzo and Raboso del Piave, and French imports that date back to the 19th century and have become assimilated into local wine-making. These are the familiar names of Cabernet (unless specified as Cabernet Sauvignon this is the more earthy Cabernet Franc that produces wines reminiscent of the Cabernets of the Loire) and Merlot. As always in the north-east there is a fair amount of the white workhorse grape of the Veneto and Friuli, Tocai.

The universal red is Merlot. In fact Merlot from the Veneto can be found on sale in most supermarkets in northern Italy, from Piedmont to Friuli. It's an extremely easy grape to grow and vinify. It can be grown happily in the plains on an industrial scale, and the wine itself is smooth and easy to drink. There are a few producers who make upmarket versions of this wine, but they are generally to be found in Friuli rather than in the Veneto.

Strada del Vino Rosso: the route

This route is only loosely based on the signposted route because experience shows that the signposts cannot always be trusted to be consecutive.

From Treviso take the road to Oderzo with perhaps a diversion before crossing the Piave to Monastier to see the superb Benedictine monastery. The Piave has strong associations with World War I and near Fossalta at Fagarè the Military Memorial recalls the battle of June 1918.

Once on the other side of the Piave head for Oderzo, an ancient town

Treviso has a picturesque Old Town, and is intersected by numerous canals.

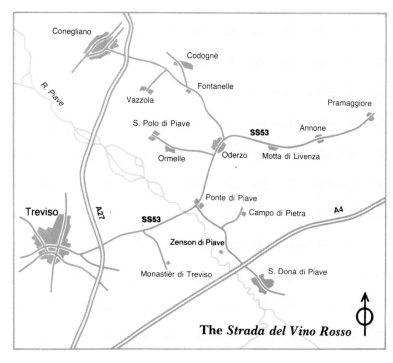

The Strada del Vino Rosso

that has been rebuilt many times after successive wars. Just on its outskirts is the enormous Consorzio Cantine Sociali della Marca Trevigiana, which stores and bottles the wine from surrounding co-operatives.

From Oderzo go east to the small town of Pramaggiore, the site of an Enoteca Nazionale, as well as being on the *Strada dei Vini Lison-Pramaggiore*. This is where one of the two important Italian wine-tasting competitions (the other is in Torgiano in Umbria) takes place every spring. An *Oscar d'Oro* at Pramaggiore is quite an achievement.

Alternatively, from Oderzo go to San Polo di Piave. This is a famous fishery whose gastronomic speciality is eel and red prawns in a green sauce. An idea of the antiquity of this tradition can be seen in the nearby church of San Giorgio at Ormelle,

where a mediaeval fresco shows a Last Supper with red prawns. On the other route to Conegliano from Oderzo there are two fine villas to see at Codognè and Fontanelle.

Breganze: *Strada del Vino*

Just north of Vicenza, near some of the finest Venetian villas (don't miss the frescoed Castello di Thiene), is the ancient town of Breganze. This is the centre of a D.O.C. wine zone with a signposted *strada del vino* system that runs through some attractive hilly countryside from Caltrano in the East to Marsan in the West.

There are seven wines of Breganze. The leading producer responsible for the fame of Breganze abroad is Fausto Maculan, whose non-D.O.C. wine Torcolato is a rival to the finest French Sauternes. Breganze has a lively wine festival every year in May (see page 63).

BREGANZE
Az. Agr. Maculan Via Castelletto 3. Tel: 0445 873733 (Fausto Maculan). All year except Aug and last week Dec. T. E. Fr. TF. WS.
Cantina B. Bartolomeo da Breganze Via Roma 100. Tel: 0445 873112 (Dr Andrea Bottaro). All year except Aug. T. E. TF. WS.

PRAMAGGIORE
Enoteca Regionale Veneto Mostra Nazionale Vini, Via Cavalieri di Vittorio Veneto 13. Tel: 0421 799036. Weekdays and Sat 0900–1200, 1500–1800. Closed Apr and May. ER. TP. WS. Guided tours of cellars in July and Aug.

For further addresses, see p.62

Treviso – the White Wine Roads

CORTINA D'AMPEZZO
Enoteca Cortina Via del Mercato 5 (and Via dei Marangoni 59). Daily 1000–1300, 1600–2100. Closed Sun.

PONTE NELLE ALPI
Enoteca alle Schiette Via Ponte delle Schiette 42. Daily 0800–0100. Closed Mon.

SCOMIGO DI CONEGLIANO
Az. Agr. Antica Quercia Via Cal. di Sopra 8. Tel: 0438 788053. Wed and Fri 1400–1600. T. TP. WS.
Cantina Zardetto Via Marcorà 15/a. Tel: 0438 788177. T. TP. WS.

SUSEGANA
Museo della Vita Agricola e del Vino Via Barriera. Tel: 0438 61060. 0900–1200,1400–2000. Closed Mon.

The **Strada del Vino Bianco**

Conegliano, the birthplace of the 16th-century artist G.B. Cima, is equally important as a city of wine. The two Treviso province *Strada del Vino* systems meet here; this is the site of the famous School of Viticulture and Oenology (wine-making studies), founded in 1877, and an Experimental Institute. There is also an exhibition of Grappa every year.

Vino Bianco

Every bar in Conegliano serves the universal white wine of the Treviso area, Prosecco. Until recently this normally sparkling white was not exported at all. It can be found as still, as *frizzante* or as a Spumante; dry and *amabile* versions are made, but none is as dry as the French *brut*.

There are certain Prosecco wine producers who have promoted the quality of their wines and now command high prices: Canevel and Mionetto are two of these.

Strada del Vino Bianco

Back in 1960 the *Strada del Vino Prosecco*, which is the more exact name of the *Strada del Vino Bianco*, was the first to be created in Italy. It winds its way from the hills of Conegliano to the hills of Valdobbiádene at the foot of the Venetian pre-Alps. It has always been a tourist area and *mescite* or Botteghe (similar to *osterie*), with signs outside which proclaim them as authorized Botteghe, serve typical food and wine. From Conegliano

VENEGAZZU DEL MONTELLO
Az. Agr. Conte Loredan Gasparini Via Martignago Alto 23. Tel: 0423 871742 (Signor Barzan). All year except Aug. t (2 days in advance). E. TF. WS. Near Villa Loredan Gasparini.
Montelvini SpA Via Cal Trevigiana 51. Tel: 0423 620292. E. TF. WS. Minimum 20 visitors. Small museum.
Vic Tesser, Galleria dei Vini Via Spineda. Tel: 0423 871400. Open shop hours. E. WS.

take the detour south via Collalbrigo and Paré to the Wine and Country Life Museum, *Museo della Vita Agricola e del Vino* at Barriera near Susegna.

Rejoin the main route and proceed to S. Pietro di Feletto for views over the hills at the Pieve. There is also a well-known Romanesque church which stands on the site of an ancient pagan temple and has a wealth of painting, with 11th to 14th-century frescoes inside.

Refróntolo has the charming Mulinetto (little mill) della Croda in a quiet valley; Solighetto and Soligo are two important wine centres; Col San Martino has an annual wine festival and the Chiesetta di San Vigillio gives views over the plains of Montello to the south.

Back to Conegliano or Treviso

Returning south from Valdobbiádene it is well worth crossing the Piave near Montebelluna. Here in the Montello is a rich wine-producing area: Montelvini, Venegazzù and the Cantina Sociale are all reputable producers. Make sure you visit Vic Tesser, an Italian expatriate returned from Australia, at the Galleria dei Vini Venegazzù, just outside Montebelluna.

You can taste a variety of the local wines and hear the wines being discussed with a knowledgeable Australian accent. The wines of the Venegazzù company, formerly the property of Count Loredan Gasparini are world famous. Taste the red Venegazzù della Casa.

Valdobbiádene, at the end of the Strada del Vino Bianco, lies on the slopes of the Venetian pre-Alps. This is the zone of Superiore di Cartizze, a much-prized Prosecco.

CANEVEL

PROSECCO

Prosecco di Valdobbiadene
denominazione di origine controllata
vino spumante fermentazione naturale
prodotto e imbottigliato da Canevel srl
Santo Stefano di Valdobbiadene · Italia
75cl · 11.5% vol.

Food and Festivals

FURTHER ADDRESSES

VALPOLICELLA

ARBIZZANO DI VALPOLICELLA
Az. Agr. Le Ragose
Loc. Le Ragose. Tel: 045 7513241. All year. T. E. G. TF. WS.

FUMANE
Az. Agr. Allegrini
Loc. Corte Giara. Tel: 045 7701138 (Marilisa Allegrini). All year except Aug. T. E. TF. WS. Minimum 10 visitors.

PEDEMONTE
Az. Agr. Flli Tedeschi snc Via Giuseppe Verdi 4. Tel: 045 7701487 (Antonietta Tedeschi). All year except Sept 20–Oct 30. T. E. TF. WS. Small groups.

TREVISO

CAMPO DI PIETRA
Az. Agricola Cescon Via Arzeri 22. Tel: 0422 744152. Weekday office hours. T. TP. WS.

RONCADE
Az. Agr. Castello di Roncade Via Roma 141. Tel: 0422 708736. All year. T. E. G. Fr. Sp. TF. WS. Magnificent castle/villa. Also Agriturismo.

FOOD SPECIALITIES

Polenta is absolutely universal in north-east Italy. This is a yellow maize flour which is boiled and then made into a cake that can be baked or fried; it takes a little getting used to and is truly delicious only if cooked with expertise by a local chef. It usually accompanies strong meats with rich sauces, such as rabbit, guinea fowl or pheasant.

Another universal dish of the Veneto is *risi bisi*, a risotto made with rice and peas, again of peasant origin. Nearly all traditional first courses are equally filling: *pasta e fagioli* (bean and pasta soup), for example, and *zuppa di trippa* (tripe soup). A legacy of pre-refrigerator days is the speciality of Vicenza, *baccalà alla vicentina*, salt cod simmered in milk and onions with the possible addition of tomatoes.

'The Rose of Chioggia' is another name for the *radicchio* plant that is used for many purposes near Treviso: in salads, grilled with pasta and even as a flavouring for Grappa.

By the Adriatic they are especially proud of their seafood. Some of the more usual fish dishes are:
Zuppa di pesce: fish soup.
Insalata di mare: mixed salad of seafood.
Seppie alla Veneziana: squid stewed in its own ink and served with pasta or with *polenta*.
Coda di Rospo: monkfish tail, usually grilled.

Strangely, the Venetians are not known so much for particular fish dishes, as for *Fegato alla Veneziana*, calves liver cooked in butter with onions.

FESTIVALS

Treviso

February: VENICE: the Carnival, famous for masked entertainers.
March: SANTO STEFANO DE VALDOBBIADENE: exhibition and tasting of Prosecco and Cartizze.
March, 2nd and 3rd week: VIDOR: patronal festival, celebrating the town's patron saint, San Giuseppe – and a wine festival.
Last week March/first week April: COL SAN MARTINO: Provincial Exhibition of Prosecco.
Easter (about two weeks after): SAN PIETRO DE BARBOZZA: exhibition and tasting of Prosecco and Cartizze.
Last week April, first week May: GUIA: Prosecco Festival.
April 25 to second week May: REFRONTOLO: Prosecco and Marzemino Festival.
May, between the last two Sundays: BREGANZE: Maggio Breganzese, wine festival.
May, first half: SAN PIETRO DE FELETTO: Prosecco Festival.
May: VENICE: Festival of the Sensa – the famous Wedding of the Sea.
July: VENICE: Feast of the Redeemer, celebrates the end of the 1576 plague.
September: MONTEBELLUNA: exhibition of D.O.C. wines from Montello and Colli Asolani.
September, first half: VALDOBBIADENE: National Exhibition of Spumante, Villa dei Cedri.
September, second and third Sundays: FARRA DI SOLIGO: Wine Festival.
October: TREVISO: Fiera di San Luca.
October: VENICE: the Regatta.
November: VENICE: Feast of the Madonna della Salute.
December: TREVISO: Festival of the Radicchio Rosso.

Padua and Vicenza

March: VICENZA: national exhibition of D.O.C. and D.O.C.G. wines.

March/April: CINTO EUGANEO: exhibition and tasting of wines from the Colli Euganei.

August: ESTE: festival of wines of the Colli Euganei.

September: ALTAVILLA VICENTINO: festival of *baccalà* (a fish speciality of the Vicenza area).

October/November: MONTEBELLO VICENTINO: festival of food and wines from the Colli Bertici.

Verona

Mid April: VERONA: VINITALY Wine Fair, public may pay to enter.

Good Friday and Easter Week: NEGRAR DI VALPOLICELLA: *Palio del Recioto* – a week-long fair with a presentation to the best Recioto-making company.

May: CAVAION: asparagus festival with tastings of local wine.

May: ILLASI: festival of Valpolicella.

May: MONTEFORTE D'ALPONE: exhibition of Soave Classico.

May: RIVOLI VERONESE: asparagus and local foods festival.

May, first Sunday: SOAVE: festival of Soave Classico.

September: GAMBELLARA: festival of Gambellara and of Recioto di Gambellara.

September: SOMMACAMPAGNA: annual festival of Bianco di Custoza.

End September: SOAVE: *Fiera dell'Uva*.

End September: BARDOLINO: *Festa dell'Uva*.

Early October: FUMANE: wine festival of Valpolicella and Recioto della Valpolicella.

October: COSTERMANO: *Festa dei Tordi* (thrushes) *con Polenta*.

November: SANT'AMBROGIO DI VALPOLICELLA: festival of chestnuts, beans and wine.

Breganze's wine festival

In the week between the last two Sundays in May, the town of Breganze is given over to the traditional Maggio Breganzese, a celebration of folk culture that has its origins in May celebrations that sprang up all over Italy in the Middle Ages. The Maggio Fiorentino in Florence is perhaps the most famous of these events. The exhibition and tasting of wines that forms part of the celebrations is an opportunity for the producer and the public alike to evaluate the last year's vintage when it has not been on sale for long.

In Breganze, the six D.O.C. wines (the whites, Pinot Grigio, Pinot Bianco and Breganze Bianco – the reds, Breganze Rosso, Cabernet and Pinot Nero) are all on display for tasting and for drinking, together with local food specialities.

The actual competition at which the wines are judged takes place at the Cantina Sociale of B. Bartolomeo di Breganze, founded in 1950, to which almost all the local producers belong. Samples of wine are submitted by local wine-growers and judged anonymously. On the final Sunday of the festival, the winner's name is revealed and a *tastevin*, an essential tool of the trade, is awarded as a prize.

During the week, stalls are set up to serve local foods, and cultural and folklore events are organized. Local crafts are also on sale.

The Breganze festival is typical of many throughout Italy, especially in May or in September/October. They vary a great deal in size and importance, but they are almost always a good opportunity for the traveller to discover the hospitality for which the Italians are famous.

FURTHER INFORMATION

Associazione Consorzi Vini Vicentini D.O.C. Corso Fogazzaro 37, 36100 Vicenza. Tel: 0444 545011. For information on the Strada del Tocai Rosso (Colli Berici), Strada del Recioto (Gambellara), and Strada del Vino Breganze.

Consorzio Tutela Vini del Piave D.O.C. c/o Camera di Commercio I.A.A., Via Toniolo 2, 31100 Treviso. Tel: 0422 540801.

Consorzio per la Tutela del Vino Prosecco di Conegliano-Valdobbiádene Villa Brandolini, Via Roma 7, 31050 Solighetto. Tel: 0438 83028. For information on the Strada del Vino Prosecco (White Wine Road) and on authorized Botteghe.

Consorzio Vino D.O.C. Bardolino Piazza Matteotti, 37011 Bardolino. Tel: 045 7210820.

Consorzio Vini D.O.C. Colli Euganei Via Vescovi 35, Torreglia. Tel: 049 5211896.

Consorzio Volontario Vini D.O.C. Lison Pramaggiore Via Vittorio Veneto 13/b, 30020 Pramaggiore. Tel: 0421 79256. For information on the Strada del Vino Lison Pramaggiore and authorized Botteghe en route.

Ente Provinciale Turismo Treviso Palazzo Scotti, Via Toniolo 41, Treviso. Tel: 0422 47632. The useful booklet *Treviso e la Sua Provincia – Itinerari* is available here.

Friuli-Venezia Giulia

The inhabitants of Friuli are a mixture of Slav, Latin and Teutonic races who live peacefully in a border region which has often been the site of bitter fighting. The signs of this past are all around: Roman Aquileia, the Venetian Republic's fortress town of Palmanova; Trieste, the port of the Austro-Hungarian Empire, and the World War I battlefields at Redipúglia. But despite mass emigration after World War II and the earthquake of 1976, Friuli is now a wealthy region.

Friuli produces only 1.3 per cent of Italy's wine, but about 45 per cent of this is at D.O.C. level, a proportion only bettered by the Trentino-Alto Adige. The northern half is mountainous and unsuited to wine-making. In the South, however, there is an ancient tradition of wine-making which is epitomized by Friuli's most famous wine, one of the great wines of the 19th century still produced today, Picolit. The white wines of Friuli are considered by many experts to be the best in Italy.

The 4th-century mosaic floor of the ancient basilica in Aquileia is one of the glories of Friuli. It was rediscovered by accident in 1909.

Although the wine industry here is small, the focus is on quality. In the 19th century, new grapes were introduced, Cabernet, Sauvignon and Riesling, for example, and today Friuli's wines have a reputation for excellence.

There are seven distinct D.O.C. regions: Grave, Collio, Colli Orientali, Latisana, Aquileia, Isonzo, and Carso. Most of them produce the same wide range of wines, but there are notable exceptions – for example, Picolit is mainly produced in Colli Orientali. The reds are Merlot (predominantly), Cabernet, Refosco, Pinot Nero, Tazzelenghe, Terrano, Schioppettino, and Malbeck. The whites are Tocai Friulano (predominantly), Pinot Bianco, Pinot Grigio, Verduzzo, Sauvignon, Malvasia, Riesling, Traminer, Picolit, and Ribolla.

Recent developments are the growth in importance of Chardonnay, soon to be D.O.C.; the increasing demand for sparkling wines; and the production of aromatic Grappas.

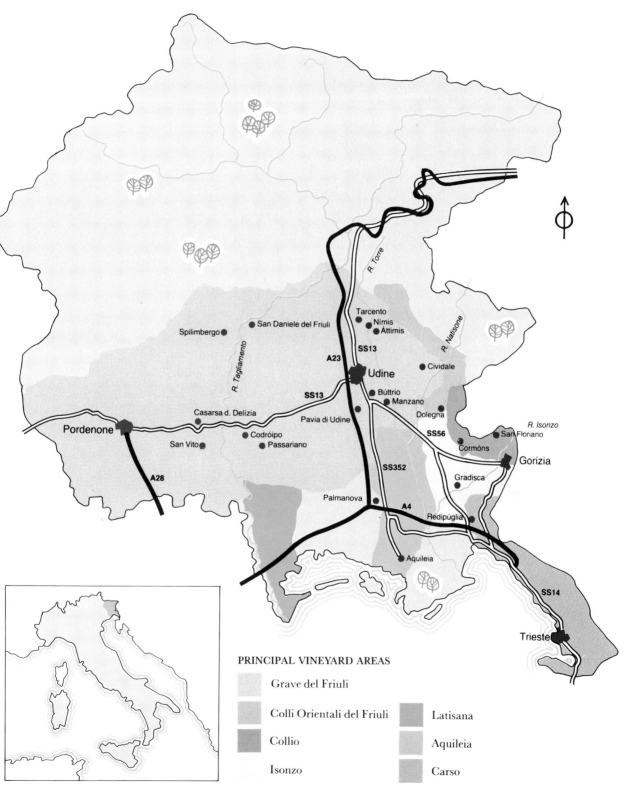

PRINCIPAL VINEYARD AREAS

Grave del Friuli

Colli Orientali del Friuli

Collio

Isonzo

Latisana

Aquileia

Carso

Udine, Grave and Colli Orientali

Grapes are harvested for Collavini, producers of the best-selling sparkling wine Il Grigio. Their wines are made from grapes from the Collio and Grave areas of Friuli.

BUTTRIO
Az. Agr. Girolamo Dorigo Via del Pozzo 3. Tel: 0432 674268 (Girolamo Dorigo, Rosetta Bosco). All year except harvest-time (about Sept 20–end Oct). T. E. TF. WS.
Az. Vit. Valle Via Nazionale 3. Tel: 0432 674289. All year. T. TF. WS. Taverna Valle attached to Cantina serves typical food.

CASARSA DELLA DELIZIA
Viticoltori Friulani la Delizia Via Udine 24. Tel: 0434 869564 (Grace Castellarin). All year except Aug. T. E. TP. WS.

Grave del Friuli: the wines
The area's name derives from the word *grave*, describing the gravelly nature of its vineyards. This is the big wine-producing area in Friuli (Pordenone has the greatest vineyard area, 5,000 hectares), and white wines predominate over reds, but only just. The most common red is the Merlot, a smooth, fruity wine. Tocai Friulano is the most common white and is also the house white of every trattoria.

Other wines likely to be encountered are Cabernet (mostly the earthy Cabernet Franc but sometimes the blackcurranty Cabernet Sauvignon), Pinot Grigio (the fashionable white), Pinot Bianco (an excellent white similar to Chardonnay), Refosco (a hearty but very quaffable red) and Verduzzo (sweet or dry white).

Grave del Friuli: the route
Enter Friuli on the SS13 through the charming riverside town of Sacile and the provincial capital Pordenone,

where you will find a wine shop Enoteca. If you can, take the time to see the paintings of Il Pordenone, Friuli's most famous artist, in the Duomo.

The biggest co-operative of Friuli, the Cantina Sociale at Casarsa, is 20km (12 miles) east of Pordenone; it produces more wine under the La Delizia trademark than the Collio.

Over the Tagliamento river at Passariano is the spectacular Villa Manin. This is where Napoleon signed the treaty that marked the end of the Venetian Republic. It is now a cultural centre owned by the local government.

North of Casarsa is Spilimbergo, which has one of the finest mediaeval churches in Friuli. Just

over the Tagliamento is the hill town of San Daniele, world famous for its *prosciutto crudo*.

Udine is a provincial capital with fascinating architecture, including a castle and Venetian Gothic and Renaissance buildings. It also has a new wine museum, the Casa del Vino, displaying all the wines of Friuli.

Colli Orientali

Some of the finest wines of Friuli are produced in this range of hills which forms an arc to the east of Udine. These same hills become the famous Collio region once they pass south into the province of Gorizia.

Twelve D.O.C. Colli Orientali wines exist at present, more whites than reds. The most famous white, the dessert wine Picolit, is a rich wine which can have a sweet or dry finish. It also has the smallest production. Tocai Friulano is the most common white. The most common red is Merlot, the least is that favourite of the Burgundians, Pinot Nero.

From Tarcento, home of the fragrant sweet white wine, Verduzzo di Ramandolo, travel south via Nimis, Attimis, and Cividale, with its 8th-century Tempietto Longobardo, then Rosazzo, with its abbey where mixed cultivation of vines and olives has been recorded since the 12th century. Manzano, and Búttrio with its Morpurgo castle, are on the way back to Udine.

il Grigio®

CODROIPO
Vigneti Pittaro Via Udine 55, Zompicchia di Codroipo. Tel: 0432 904726 (Piero Pittaro, Stefano Trinco). 0800–1200, 1400–1600. T. TF. WS. Wine museum.

PAVIA DI UDINE
Az. Agr. Fratelli Pighin Viale Grado 1, Fraz. Risano. Tel: 0432 675444 (Roberto and Livio Pighin). All year. T. E. G. TF. WS. Vineyard visit. Small groups only.

PORDENONE
Enoteca La Cheba Vicolo del Campanile 1. Tel: 0434 22628. 1000–1400, 1700–2400

S. VITO AL TAGLIAMENTO
Museo Provinciale della Vita Contadina Via Falcon Vial. T (at Biblioteca Civica, tel: 0434 80405). Small groups.

UDINE
Casa del Vino Via Poscolle 6. Tel: 0432 297068. 0830–1300, 1400–1730. Tastings for groups only. Useful information centre.

The Piazza della Libertà in Udine has an assembly of statuary dominated by an ornate clock tower dating from 1527.

Collio

CAPRIVA DEL FRIULI
**Agricola Castello di
Spessa** Via Spessa 1. Tel:
0481 80072. All year. t. TF.
WS.
**Az. Agr. Istituto 'A
Cerruti' Villa Russiz**
Russiz Inferiore 5. Tel: 0481
80047 (Dott. Gianni
Menotti). T. E. TP. WS.
Historic Villa.
Az. Agr. Russiz Superiore
Loc. Russiz Superiore.
Tel: 0481 92237 (Silvano
Burello). May-June, Oct-
Nov. T. E. G. TF.
Maximum 8 visitors.

CORMONS
**Casa Vinicola Tenuta di
Angoris** Loc. Angoris 7. Tel:
0481 60923. All year except
Aug, Dec and Jan. T. Fr. Sp.
TF. WS. Historic villa.

DOLEGNA DEL COLLIO
Ristorante da Venica Via
Mernico 37. Tel: 0481 60177.
Closed Tues. Winery, tennis,
riding.

GRADISCA D'ISONZO
**Enoteca Permanente
Regionale 'La
Serenissima'.** Tel: 0481
99528. Every day except
Mon 1000-1300, 1600-2400.
ER. TP. Displays wines
which have won the annual
Gran Premio Noè
competition.
Marco Felluga srl Via
Gorizia 121. Tel: 0481 99164
(Silvano Burello). May-June,
Oct-Nov. T. E. G. TF.
Maximum 8 visitors.

**S. FLORIANO DEL
COLLIO**
Cantina Formentini Via
Oslavia 5. 0800-1700, Sat
(and holidays) 1400-1900.
Wine museum, Enoteca,
hotel, golf course. TP. WS.

Most of the former 'Garden of the
Austro-Hungarian Empire', where
Imperial civil servants used to
holiday, is now in Yugoslavia. But
what remains is a land that produces
about 1,300 hectolitres of top quality
wine every year.

In the 1960s, the technology of
white wine-making was much
refined. As a result, the wines of the
Collio tend to be both well made and
relatively costly. As with expensive
French wines, such as white
Burgundy, whether they are good
value depends on personal taste.

White wines predominate over
reds by four to one. Tocai takes up
one third, then, in order of size of
production, Pinot Bianco, Pinot
Grigio, Sauvignon, Malvasia Istriana
and Collio Bianco. Of the reds the
most important are Merlot, Cabernet
Franc and Pinot Nero.

Generally, Collio wines are bigger,
rounder and fatter in taste than their
counterparts from the other areas of
Friuli. They are made with a slightly
higher alcoholic content and are
perfect wines for a summer evening.

Collio wines: *Strada del Vino*
A signposted *Strada del Vino* system
was set up for the Collio in 1963. It
takes in some of the most attractive
vineyard-covered hill scenery in
Italy, but it is also an area which saw
some of the fiercest fighting of World
War I – trenches are still visible in
the landscape, ammunition and
skeletons are still dug up in the
course of vineyard cultivation.

The wine route begins in Gorizia
at the Ponte del Torrione. Gorizia
itself is worth seeing for its castle,
cathedral and Museum of Folklore.
From Gorizia the route goes to
Monte Calvario with its monument
to the dead of World War I, and
Oslávia, whose cemetery contains
the bones of 60,000 Italian dead.

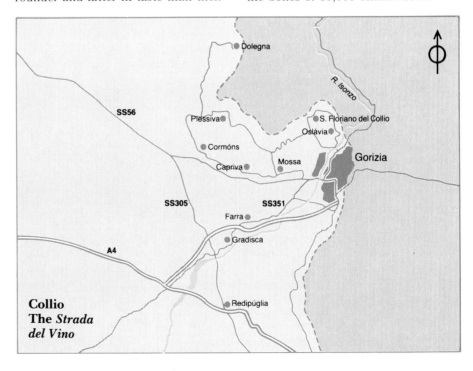

**Collio
The *Strada
del Vino***

On a hill overlooking Yugoslavia is San Floriano del Collio. The 15th-century castle at the summit belongs to one of the leading producers of the Collio, Count Michele Formentini. Here, in castle buildings that his family has owned since 1520, Count Formentini has created a complex which combines a hotel furnished with family antiques, an Enoteca for the tasting and sale of Collio wines, and a wine museum which displays traditional wine-making artefacts. The whole complex is surrounded by Formentini vineyards, and a 9-hole golf course. The Formentini have long been wine-makers; indeed, the Furmint grape of Hungarian Tokay is said to have been named after an ancestor.

From San Floriano the road follows the Yugoslav border to Plessiva. Italians can cross the border with only an identity card. In fact they are also permitted to harvest grapes from the vineyards that they still own in the Yugoslav Collio. But, somewhat absurdly, given the reputation of the Italian Collio, E.E.C. law only permits the grapes so harvested to be used for the lowly *Vino da Tavola*.

From Plessiva go to Dolegna, with perhaps lunch and a tasting at the restaurant attached to the winery of Gianni Venica. Thence to Cormóns, Capriva, and Mossa. Here, before returning to Gorizia, you should visit the Regional Enoteca at Gradisca d'Isonzo. Sited in the 15th-century house of the *Provveditori Veneti*, the Enoteca displays wines from Friuli that have won the annual Gran Premio Noè competition. It also hosts a sparkling wine exhibition every December.

Villa Russiz is surrounded by its own vineyards in the midst of the Collio country. This is the most prestigious vineyard area in Friuli.

Friuli – the Coastal Plains

The Adriatic coast of Friuli includes the three D.O.C. wine areas of Latisana, Aquileia and, near Trieste, the Carso. Inland at the foot of the Collio are the D.O.C. lands of the Isonzo river. Each of these areas has its own wine characteristics.

Latisana

Just over the border from the Veneto in the south-western part of Friuli is Latisana. As a town it is not particularly interesting, but as a D.O.C. wine-making area which includes the flat land bordering the Tagliamento river on the Friuli side it is worthy of note.

The wines are more honest than exciting, but good examples of standard Friuli favourites, such as the whites Tocai and Pinot Bianco and the red Cabernet, can be found. Two thirds of Latisana wines are red, one third is white.

A route around the vineyards might start at Latisana, go north to Varmo, east to Rivignano and descend again, via Precenicco to the seaside resort of Lignano Sabbiadoro.

Aquileia

The other side of the lagoon from Lignano is the D.O.C. area of Aquileia.

Aquileia itself is a Roman town and mediaeval patriarchate whose cathedral has important 4th-century mosaics (see photograph, page 64). Grado, the old port for Aquileia and the town the inhabitants of Aquileia fled to after the collapse of Roman rule, is also worth visiting.

Red wines predominate here. Refosco is a personal favourite, but almost the whole range of Friulan wine types can be found somewhere in the area.

A tour of the wine-producing area might start at Cervignano del Friuli, go north to the Venetian fortress town of Palmanova, go east to S. Vito al Torre and descend to Aquileia and Grado via the town of Ruda.

Carso: *Strada del Terrano*

The Carso is a new D.O.C. area created in 1985. It is named after the particular geological feature, *carsismo*, which means that water has carved out underground caverns and tunnels in the rock. The most obvious effect of this can be seen at S. Giovanni al Timavo where the river suddenly bubbles up to the surface after 38km (24 miles) underground.

The two wines of the region are Malvasia Istriana and Terrano, the traditional table wine of Trieste that is incidentally reputed to be good for the blood. A *Strada del Vino* system has recently been set up with signposted roads that cover the area

A cypress-lined street in old Roman Aquileia is part of the remains of a city founded in 181 BC. In Roman times, Aquileia was one of the principal towns of north-east Italy.

bounded by Monrupino, Sgonicó and Duino Aurusina.

The Carso being an exposed strip of Italy next to Yugoslavia, much of it is under military jurisdiction.

Isonzo: *Strada del Merlot*

The D.O.C. Isonzo area lies in the river valley at the foot of the more famous wine-producing area of the Collio hills.

The Isonzo has a 40km (25 mile) *Strada del Merlot* which takes in vineyards not only of the area's best wine, Merlot, but also of the white wines Riesling Italico and Traminer. It starts at Gradisca d'Isonzo, whose Enoteca Regionale is a must to visit on the wine tour of Friuli (see pages 68–69), and goes on to Romans, Fratta, Medea, Borgnano, Angoris, Cormons, Brazzano, Mariano, Corona and San Lorenzo Isontino.

Excursions in this area might include the Military Museum at San Michele, near the memorial at Redipúglia, and the fortress town of Palmanova.

LATISANA

Az. Agr. Zaglia Viale Stazione 18. Tel: 0431 50087 (Giorgio Zaglia). Office hours. T. TP. WS.

PALAZZO DELLA STELLA

Az. Agr. Isola Augusta Loc. Isola Augusta. Tel: 0431 58046. Weekdays 0900–1200. t. TP. WS.

TRIESTE

Enoteca Bere Bene Viale Ippodromo 2/3. Tel: 040 390965. 0830–1300, 1530–1900 (1600–1930 in summer). Closed Sun and Mon.
Enoteca Bischoff Via Mazzini 21. Tel: 040 392277. 0830–1300, 1530–1900. Closed Mon.

Villa Manin at Passariano (see page 66) once the residence of Venice's last Doge, now houses an institute for research into Friuli's cultural heritage.

Food and Festivals

FURTHER INFORMATION

Azienda Regionale per la Promozione Turistica del Friuli-Venezia Giulia Via Rossini 6, 34132 Trieste. Tel: 040 60336. Booklet *Lo Scopriregione A guide for a different day* available.
Camera di Commercio I.A.A. Via Morpurgo 4, 33100 Udine. Tel: 0432 504541. Booklet *The wines of Friuli* available.
Centro Regionale Potenziamento Viticoltura e dell'Enologia del Friuli-Venezia Giulia Via Vittorio Veneto 65, 33100 Udine. Tel: 0432 297068. Booklet *Friuli-Venezia Giulia, The Golden Land* available.
Consorzio Tutela Denominazione Origine Vini Collio Via C. Battisti 10, 34071 Cormons. Tel: 0481 630303.
Consorzio Volontario Tutela dei Vini D.O.C. Grave del Friuli c/o Camera di Commercio I.A.A., Corso Vittorio Emanuele 47, 33170 Pordenone. Tel: 0434 208476.

OSTERIA AND *FRASCA*

To explore the riches of Friulan cuisine it is essential to discover the *frasca* and the *osteria*.

The *osteria* can be found in most parts of Italy, but perhaps it is here that it comes closest to the original idea of an all-day convivial meeting place where you can have a snack and glass of wine or beer at any time. There is in fact a Committee for the Defence of the Friulan *osteria*.

The *frasca*, or *mescita*, is a more impromptu and seasonal outdoor *osteria*, which mainly occurs in the two to three months around spring. Throughout the wine-producing areas *frasche* will suddenly emerge in the courtyards of farmhouses. A few rickety chairs and tables may be set outside, and you can have a plate of the typical homemade farmhouse salami and cheese products with a glass of the new season's wine for a modest sum.

FOOD SPECIALITIES

The Friulan gastronomic tradition is a very varied one. Slav, Italian and Germanic styles are used to prepare the different foods available from the sea, hills and mountains.

The most famous food to come from Friuli is the *prosciutto crudo* of San Daniele. A recipe book published in 1450, written by Mastro Martino, the chef of the Patriarch of Aquileia, reveals how to test the readiness of this ham by plunging a knife into its centre. Nothing much has changed except that nowadays they use a fine horsebone for the same purpose. More unusual than the San Daniele ham is that of Sauris, which is

FESTIVALS

Friuli Festivals
More formal festivals in Friuli include the following:
February: GRADISCA D'ISONZO: exhibition of *barrique* wines.
End March: GRADISCA D'ISONZO: week-long festival of wines of the Carso.
End April: CASARSA DELLA DELIZIA: festival of wine and Friulan folklore.
End April: AQUILEIA: wine festival.
End April: BUTTRIO: regional wine exhibition.
End April: S. FLORIANO DEL COLLIO: Tasting and Exhibition of Collio Wines.
End May: CIVIDALE DEL FRIULI: exhibition of D.O.C. wines.
End May: GRADISCA D'ISONZO: exhibition of wines and *Gran Premio Noè*, the most important wine competition of Friuli and the one that decides which wines will be exhibited at the Enoteca Regionale at Gradisca.

another *prosciutto crudo* made from a rare breed of Friulan pig.

The Friulani are fond of soups; *jota* is the traditional soup of Trieste; *pasta con fagioli* soups are common, as is *brovada* (broth).

Rice is normally found in the coastal regions, and is used to make exquisite fish risottos. Other Friulan dishes include: *Cialzon* – each region has its own filling (rarely meat) of this traditional ravioli; *Muset* – the pasta *cotechino* is aged for about a month (hence its name, deriving from *mesetto*), and is often served in soup as a *Brovada di Muset*; and *Gulyas* – a goulash.

July: CORMONS: wine festival.
August: SACILE: wine festival.
August: SAN DANIELE DEL FRIULI:
Prosciutto Festival.
September: CORMONS, RASPANO-
CASSACO, POVOLETTO: *Festa dell'Uva.*
October: GRADISCA D'ISONZO: regional
exhibition of Grappa.

November: S. GIUSEPPE DELLA CHIUSA,
RICMANJE, S. DORLIGO DELLA VALLE:
Mostra Assaggio del Vino Nuovo, tasting
of the new season's wine.
November: ROMANS D'ISONZO: tasting,
exhibition of Collio and Isonzo wine.
December: GRADISCA D'ISONZO:
exhibition of sparkling wines.

*Italians are acknowledged
leaders in the field of bottle and
label design. Heavy opaque
bottles with deep 'punts' give a
touch of special elegance to the
wine. (The punt is the
indentation in the centre of the
base – a feature associated with
champagne and other fine wines
from France.)*

73

The Via Emilia

The Roman road of the Via Emilia unites the prosperous cities of Emilia Romagna. Every one is worth a visit, for the frescoes, statues and mosaics in their baptisteries and churches. Parma and Modena have very fine mediaeval and modern buildings; the Teatro Farnese in Parma and the Galleria Estense in Modena are worth seeing. Bologna is famous for its many towers, its university, and, of course, for its wonderful food. Faenza has a museum of the decorated ceramic ware that bears its name, while the ancient mosaics of Ravenna, for a time the capital of the Roman Empire after the fall of Rome, should not be missed on any account. Dante's tomb is also in Ravenna; and Garibaldi's hut in the woods, where he hid before escaping to America, can also be visited. Ferrara bears many reminders of a splendid cultural past when great Renaissance poets and painters came to the court of the Este. But there is also a special ambience to the towns and the countryside. Anyone who has seen *The Garden of the Finzi-Contini* or Bertolucci's *1900* will already have a good idea of the region's atmosphere.

Unfortunately, the region is associated with its great export, the notorious cheap party wine, Lambrusco, and amongst its other wines there are no real stars. But, on its home ground, Lambrusco is in fact quite different. It is a great peasant wine, and it expresses in its instant earthy drinkability the first reason for drinking wine at all – for refreshment.

Wine is produced in all eight provinces of Emilia Romagna. The majority comes from the large co-operatives of Forlì, Bologna and Ravenna. But the best wine comes from individual producers.

Of the most commonly found reds, the best are Gutturnio from Colli Piacentini, Lambrusco from Sorbara, and Sangiovese di Romagna. Of the whites, look out for the Sauvignon and the sparkling Malvasia from Colli di Parma, which can be both a dry aperitif wine or an excellent sweet dessert wine. Albana has now been given the prestigious D.O.C.G. *appellation*.

The Passatore, a Robin Hood-like character, has become the trademark of Romagna's wines (see page 78).

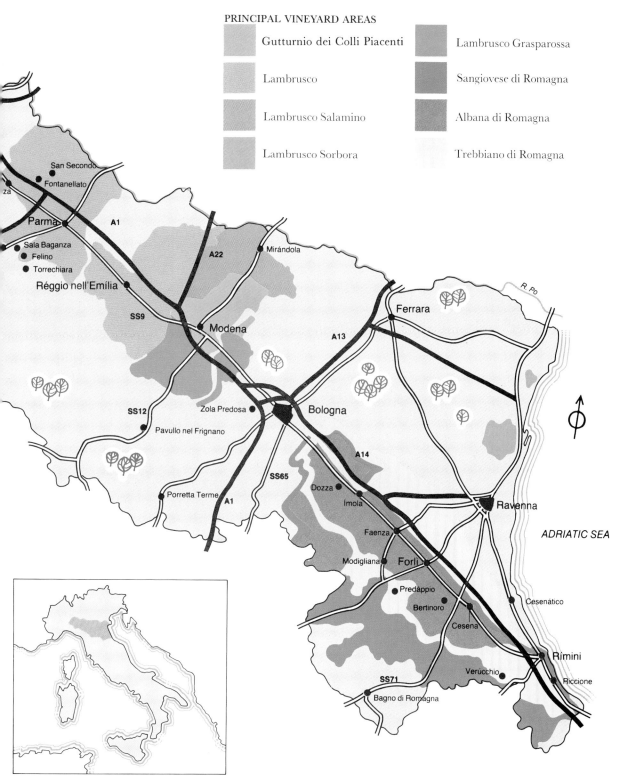

PRINCIPAL VINEYARD AREAS

Gutturnio dei Colli Piacenti

Lambrusco

Lambrusco Salamino

Lambrusco Sorbora

Lambrusco Grasparossa

Sangiovese di Romagna

Albana di Romagna

Trebbiano di Romagna

San Secondo
Fontanellato
za
Parma
A1
Sala Baganza
Felino
Torrechiara
Réggio nell'Emília
SS9
SS12
Pavullo nel Frignano
Porretta Terme
A1
Mirándola
A22
Modena
A13
Zola Predosa
Bologna
SS65
Dozza
Ímola
Faenza
Modigliana
Forli
Predáppio
Bertinoro
Cesena
SS71
Bagno di Romagna
Verúcchio
Ferrara
R. Po
A14
Ravenna
ADRIATIC SEA
Cesenático
Rímini
Riccione

Wines of the Via Emilia

Barbera and Bonarda, and the white Malvasia. This last-named wine can be sweet or dry, and still or sparkling, and it is the standard white of all Emilia Romagna.

The most interesting red, Gutturnio, comes from the hills between Castel San Giovanni and Pianello in the west and around the mediaeval town of Castel l'Arquato in the south. Gutturnio, named after the Roman drinking vessel found near Piacenza in 1878, is a smooth blend of Barbera and Bonarda.

Turning south-west to Bóbbio, travel down the Val Trebbia, with its own tongue-twisting white wine, Trebbianino. Bóbbio has an Enoteca and restaurant in the 17th-century former church of San Nicola. The basilica of Bóbbio is the resting place of Saint Colomba.

Emilia-Romagna's wines include the famous Lambrusco, while Fattoria Paradiso has captured the spirit of good drinking in Romagna.

BERTINORO
Fattoria Paradiso Via Palmiggiana 285. Tel: 0543 445044 (Marco Lorenzini). All year. E. Fr. TF. WS. Museum. Enoteca.

BOBBIO
Enoteca San Nicola Contrada dell'Ospedale. Tel: 0523 932355. All day. Closed Thurs and Nov.

DOZZA
Enoteca Regionale Emilia-Romagna Rocca Sforzesca. Tel: 0542 678089. Winter 1000–1200, 1400–1700, summer 1000–1200, 1500–1800. Closed Mon. ER. TP. WS. Sited in mediaeval castle.

PARMA
Antica Osteria Fontana Via Farini 24/A. Tel: 0521 286037. 0900–1500, 1630–2100. Closed Sun.

Almost the entire length of the Roman Via Emilia is a wine-producing area.

Around Piacenza
Wine is produced in the hilly areas, the Colli Piacentini. The most notable are the quaffable reds,

Around Parma
Lambrusco derives from the Latin for a wild vine, Lambrusca, and it is from the plains around Parma that this fizzy red wine comes. It is delicious chilled and served with the other famous products of Parma, Parma ham and parmesan. Visit the beautiful moated and frescoed 15th-century castle of Fontanellato.

San Secondo is famous for its cured meat, Spalla di San Secondo. A perfect match is the local red wine, Fortana. South of Parma are the vineyards for the little known Colli di Parma wines. Try the white Malvasia, the Sauvignon, and Colli di Parma Rosso, which is a blend of Barbera and Bonarda similar to Gutturnio.

A drive in the Parma hills might take in the *cru* areas of Sala Baganza, Felino, and Torrechiara, which has a well-preserved mediaeval castle.

Around Modena

There are no fewer than three types of Lambrusco to be found around Modena: Sorbara, S. Croce and Castelvetro. If drunk cellar cool and from a reputable producer, such as Cavicchioli, it is an undemanding and refreshing wine.

Bologna

Bologna is the acknowledged gastronomic capital of Italy, but it is only in the Colli Bolognesi to the south of the city that there is any wine of note. Here it is mostly wines made from single-grape varieties that are produced; the most famous producer is Enrico Vallania of Terre Rosse at Zola Predosa.

The Romagna

Between Bologna and the Adriatic coast is the Romagna. Principal wines are: Sangiovese di Romagna, a light red with a pleasant bitter twist to its aftertaste; Albana di Romagna, a white which can be sweet, dry, still or sparkling and has been awarded the prestigious D.O.C.G., although the quality still seems very variable; white Trebbiano di Romagna; red Cagnina di Romagna; and Pagadebit, white and grassy.

The wine route begins at Dozza, near Imola just south of the Via Emilia. The castle here is the site of the Regional Enoteca.

There are diversions possible from Faenza to Marzeno di Faenza, Marzeno di Brisighella, and Modigliana.

From Forlì, with its Ethnographic Museum, turn south to the Enoteca and museum of the Zoli family Cantina at Predáppio Alta. Or continue further down the Via Emilia and visit the attractive hilly area of Bertinoro, with its Enoteca and also Mario Pezzi's famous Fattoria Paradiso.

The Via Emilia reaches the Adriatic coast at the holiday town of Rimini where there is an Enoteca Ristorante. Further north in historic Ravenna there is an Enoteca near Dante's tomb, and in Ferrara there is an *osteria* and Enoteca that can trace its history of hospitality back to 1435 (see page 78).

VILLA VERUCCHIO
Tenuta Amalia Gebo Via Molino Bianco 734. Tel: 0541 678538. All year. T. Fr. Sp. TF. WS. Former residence of Caroline of Brunswick, wife of George IV of England.

Parma's cathedral has an immense late 12th/early 13th-century Baptistery, with monumental sculpted portals.

Food and Festivals

VINI DEL PASSATORE

Enoteche to visit

The wines of Romagna are promoted by the Ente Tutela dei Vini Romagnoli, which uses as its trademark the bearded figure of a *passatore*, the gentleman bandit of the 18th and 19th centuries, part of the folklore of the once lawless Romagna region. The Ente Tutela also sponsors four Enoteche, in which it is possible to taste their approved wines together with typical local foods. The four have dialect names and are: Ca' da Be' in Bertinoro, which looks out over the plain to the Adriatic (museum attached); Ca' da Ve'n in Ravenna, near the tomb of Dante in an old palazzo; Ca' de Sanzves in Predáppio Alta, the ancient Cantina of the Zoli family, traditional wine-makers of the area (museum attached); and Enoteca Ristorante Chesa de Vein in Rimini.

FOOD SPECIALITIES

It is Emilia rather than Romagna that is the gastronomic centre of Italy. But, as always with Italy, the same foods are served with local variations throughout the region and individual towns have their own claims to fame. What is known as *cappelletti* in one town may appear as *agnoli, anolini, cappellacci, tortelli, tortellini, tortelloni* or *rivoltoni* in another. Indeed, what is *agnolotti* in Piedmont is *panzerotti* in the Veneto and *tortelloni* in Emilia. But whatever the name, the stuffed pasta of Emilia is superb, and the quality of the meat and dairy products ensures that this culinary tradition continues.

Apart from Browning's dramatic poem *My Last Duchess* and Parma

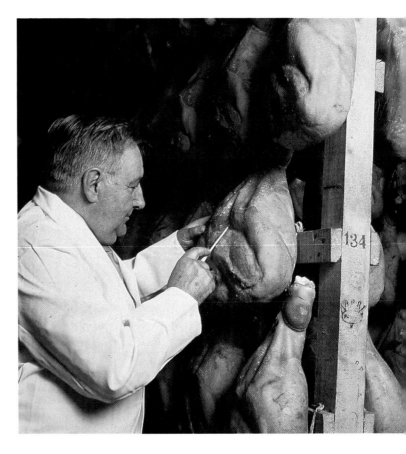

Violets, the associations of Parma are with food. Parma ham, *prosciutto crudo di Parma*, is as world famous as parmesan (though not all lovers of that unique cheese appreciate that *parmigiano* is just the most expensive of a range of similar hard cheeses, called *grana*, which are made all over the Po valley).

Bolognese gastronomy

Bologna is Italy's gastronomic capital; all Italians will tell you that their gastronomic dream is to go to one of the better restaurants of Bologna. A simple plateful of *Tortelloni alla Bolognese* served with just a flake of fresh local butter and some freshly grated parmesan, can make the most memorable of meals.

The famous Prosciutto di Parma is tested for maturity by piercing with a bone blade. Italians regard the Prosciutto di San Daniele, in Friuli, as even better (see page 67).

FURTHER INFORMATION

Consorzio Tutela Vino D.O.C. Lambrusco di Modena Viale Martiri della Libertà 28, Modena. Tel: 059 235005.
Ente Provinciale Turismo Parma Piazza Duomo 5, Parma. Tel: 0521 33959. *Parma, Vini e Luoghi* booklet available.
Ente Tutela Vini Romagnoli Corso Garibaldi 2, 48018 Faenza. Tel: 0546 28455. *Passatore Wines* booklet available.

Other local foods

Coppa: this is a dried and cured meat made from the neck and shoulders of the pig. It is eaten thinly sliced with bread and butter.

Felino: reckoned to be the finest salami of Emilia Romagna.

Stuffed pig's trotter, *Zampone di Modena*: can now be bought foil-wrapped in many delicatessens. Contrary to the name, its origins are in Emilia.

Mortadella: the huge and soft spiced pink sausage made from pork (all parts), now so famous as to have its cut price imitations. The genuine product is very good. As is the case with most sausages, it is probably best not to ponder too much on the exact ingredients.

FESTIVALS

May: BOLOGNA: procession of the Madonna of St Luke. The holy statue is returned to its traditional sanctuary after one week in the Cathedral.

End May: FERRARA: Palio of St George.

June: SORAGNA (Parma): Culatello and Fortana Wine Fair, a festival celebrating regional salami and local wines.

End June: FAENZA (Ravenna): Palio del Niballo. Costume festival.

June/July: BRISIGHELLA (Ravenna): mediaeval festival, with theatre, music and dance.

September: BAZZANO and MONTE SAN PIETRO: *Sagra dell'uva*. Food and wine festivals.

October: COTIGNOLA: festival of wines from Romagna.

New Year's Eve: FAENZA (Ravenna): *La Nott del Bisò*. Mulled wine, salami and local *dolci*.

The Regional Enoteca at Dozza in Emilia-Romagna is splendidly housed in a mediaeval fortress and dedicated to the display and tasting of wines from throughout the region. Dozza is the start of the local wine route.

Enoteca Regionale di Emilia-Romagna Rocca Sforzesca, 40050 Dozza. Tel: 0542 678089.

Tuscany

For many of its visitors, Tuscany is Italy. Indeed this is the geographic and cultural centre of Italy and once, from 1864 to 1871, it was the political centre too. But most of all Tuscany is Grand Tour country: few cities in the world can compare with Florence in its wealth of art and brilliant architecture; Siena is smaller, but extraordinarily rich in mediaeval treasures; and the little hilltop town of San Gimignano is a perfectly preserved picture of mediaeval life. Less obvious are the industries of Tuscany: the marble of Carrara, Prato's textiles, Val d'Elsa furniture, Florentine leather goods, jewellery, and so on.

Tourism is still central, of course. There are hordes in Florence, and there is a small invasion of wealthy northern Europeans who have bought cottages in the countryside. And just as Florence often represents Italian culture, Chianti is the one Italian wine that everyone has heard of. In fact the typical Chianti *fiasco* with its woven straw covering could almost serve as a symbol for the international idea of an Italian restaurant.

The dome with a view is a technical and artistic masterpiece by the early Renaissance architect Brunelleschi. It crowns Florence's cathedral.

Once notorious for its unreliable wine, Tuscany is now the most dynamic wine-producing area of Italy. Such is the pace of change in Tuscan wine-making that a new breed of wines has recently emerged, high price, high quality, non-D.O.C. wines with fantasy names: Concerto, Sassicaia, Vigorello, Tignanello, to name but a few.

Traditional Tuscan reds include the most expensive Italian wine, Brunello di Montalcino; Vino Nobile di Montepulciano; Chianti from a major part of the provinces of Florence and Siena as well as from the famous Chianti Classico area; Carmignano, one of the tiniest and highest quality D.O.C. areas; and other local reds such as Morellino di Scansano and Rosso delle Colline Lucchesi, rarely seen abroad.

Tuscany is not well known for its whites, but there has been a successful revival of traditional wines, such as Montecarlo and Bianco Vergine della Valdinievole. The big Chianti producers have also created a successful crisp light white called Galestro, and a light red suitable for drinking cool, Sarmento.

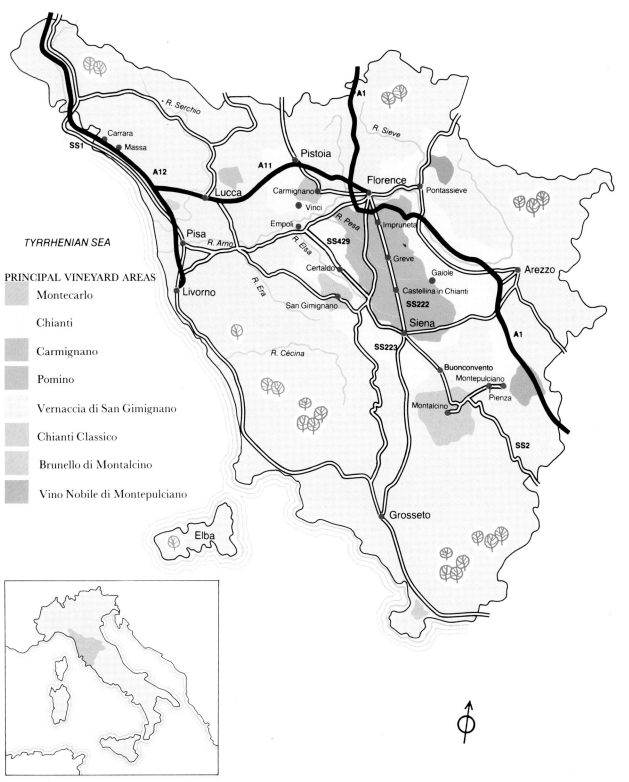

TYRRHENIAN SEA

PRINCIPAL VINEYARD AREAS

Montecarlo

Chianti

Carmignano

Pomino

Vernaccia di San Gimignano

Chianti Classico

Brunello di Montalcino

Vino Nobile di Montepulciano

From Pisa to Florence

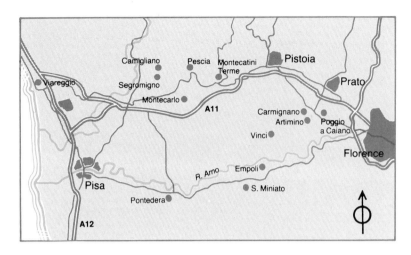

ARTIMINO
Artimino SpA Via 5
Martiri 29. Tel: 055
8718072 (Giuseppe Poggi).
All·year Sat 1530–1830,
Sun and Mon 0900–1200,
Tues-Fri 1500–1830. Closed
Aug-Oct. T. E. G. TP. WS.
On site Etruscan Museum
and Villa Medicea La
Ferdinanda.

BACCHERETO
Fattoria di Bacchereto
Via Fontemorana 179. Tel:
055 8712191 (Carlo Bencini
Tesi). Weekdays
1000–1200, 1600–1800. T.
TP. WS. Restaurant
'Cantina di Toia' attached.

MONTECARLO
**Az. Agr. Eredi
Carmignani** Via della
Tinaia Cercatoia 7. Tel:
0583 22381 (Gino
Carmignani). Weekdays.
T. TP. WS. Also
Agriturismo.
Fattoria del Buonamico
Via Provinciale di
Montecarlo 43, Loc.
Cercatoia. Tel: 0583 22038
(Franco and Vasco Grassi).
All year. t. TF. WS.

*Lucca's huge 18th-century
ramparts surround a city full
of history.*

Pisa is the normal entrance point to
Tuscany if you arrive by air, or if
you have come by train from Liguria.
This is a pleasant place to pass a few
hours, and the city centre has many
mediaeval buildings. But the Campo
Santo itself, with its world famous
Leaning Tower, the glorious marble-
faced cathedral and the highly
ornamented baptistery, is best seen
either at low season or in the small
hours of the morning, when it is not
obscured by tourists.

Lucca and the countryside
Once on the A11 motorway at Pisa,
the temptation is to head for
Florence and to ignore the
intervening towns. This is a mistake,
both in cultural and vinous terms.
Lucca is a beautiful mediaeval city
with ancient piazzas and another
splendid marble-faced cathedral.
The city can be viewed from its
ramparts, the *giro delle mura*. Its
province has two interesting wines:
Rosso delle Colline Lucchesi and
one of the most interesting Tuscan
whites, Montecarlo.

A few kilometres north of Lucca on
the SS12 a turn to the east will bring
the traveller to a series of magnificent

villas in the foothills of the
Apennines, the Colline Lucchesi,
zone of the eponymous D.O.C. red
wine. The most notable of these, both
open to the public, are Villa
Torrigiani at Camigliano and Villa
Mansi at Segromigno. Several
companies in the area are also the
producers of Rosso delle Colline
Lucchesi. Telephone in advance if
you wish to visit Fattoria Maionchi,
producers of wine and the famous
Luccan olive oil in their 18th-
century villa at Tofori.

Back towards the A11 motorway a
small D.O.C. area surrounds the
hilltop town of Montecarlo and its
mediaeval castle. Its white wine

The Medicis built the palatial Villa Artimino, one of many princely villas in the Tuscan countryside. The estate of Villa Artimino is now one of the leading producers of Carmignano.

Fattoria Michi Via San Martino 34. Tel: 0583 22011 (Piero Luciani). Weekdays and Sat 0830–1200, 1430–1800. TP. WS.

MONTELUPO FIORENTINO
Fattoria Sammontana Loc. Sammontana. Tel: 0571 542003 (Valesco Paloni). Weekdays 0900–1300, 1600–1900. T. TP. WS.

Tenuta San Vito in Fior di Selva Via San Vito / Camaioni. Tel: 0571 51411 (Mario Manenti). Sat p.m. and Sun a.m. TP. WS.

PISA
Enoteca La Limonaia Vicolo del Ruschi 2/a. Tel: 050 41535. Wine shop. Daily. Restaurant attached.

SEANO
Tenuta di Capezzana Carmignàno Tel: 055 9806005 (Beatrice, Vittorio, Ugo Contini Bonacossi). All year except Aug. T. E. Fr. WS.

TOFORI
Fattoria Maionchi. Tel: 0583 978194 (Mariapia Maionchi, Roberto Palagi). All year. T. E. Fr. TF. WS. Also olive oil. Historic 18th-century villa.

VINCI
Cantine Leonardo da Vinci Bivio di Streda. Tel: 0571 508254. All year. t. E. G. TF. WS.

(perhaps because its Trebbiano content is limited to 60–70 per cent) is one of the fruitiest and most characterful of all Tuscan whites and is just starting to become known outside its own region. Several producers welcome visitors.

Vinci and Carmignano
Leaving Pisa by the SS67 for Florence, turn northwards to Vinci for a circuitous drive through the hills and a visit with vinous interest. In Leonardo's home town there is a museum to the great artist and you can visit his birthplace. Just outside the town the wine co-operative has a small tasting and exhibition room. Their Galestro is very refreshing.

From Vinci it is a short drive over the hills to Carmignano, one of the smallest D.O.C. areas in Italy and one of Tuscany's great red wines. As long ago as 1716 Cosimo III de' Medici issued a decree delimiting the classic wine-growing areas of Carmignano which still applies

today. Indeed, several producers make a wine called Barco Reale made exclusively from grapes picked within the original, delimited, walled vineyards.

Carmignano's success lies in the addition of a barely perceptible 10 per cent of Cabernet Sauvignon (known locally as *uva francesca*, 'the French grape'), which does indeed give the wine a similarity to the classic reds of Bordeaux. Conte Ugo Contini Bonacossi of Capezzana started the annual public quality control tastings which brought Carmignano to the notice of the wine world. Both the leading producers, Tenuta di Capezzana and Artimino, are worth visiting for the architecture of their villas as well as the quality of their wines.

The SS26 leads back to Florence from Carmignano through Poggio a Caiano, also in the Carmignano D.O.C. area, but more famous for the Medici villa designed by Sangallo for Lorenzo il Magnifico.

Florence and Rùfina

FLORENCE
Bottiglieria Bussotti Via San Gallo 161r. Tel: 055 483091. 0830–1300, 1600–1930. Wine shop. Closed Sun and (p.m.) Wed.

La Cantinetta Antinori (wine bar), Palazzo Antinori. Tel: 055 292234. Mon-Fri 1200–1430, 1900–2130.

Enoteca Il Cantinone del Gallo Nero Via Santo Spirito 6r. Tel: 055 218898. 1230–1400, 1930–2230. Closed Mon and Aug. EP. Food and wine products of Chianti Classico exhibited in 15th-century palazzo.

POMINO
Marchesi de'Frescobaldi SpA Via S. Spirito 11, 50125 Firenze. Tel: 055 218751 (Signora Cristina Rinaldi, Connie Manar). All year except Aug. T. E. G. Fr. TP. Book for visits to Castello di Nipozzano (museum in 12th-century castle) and Tenuta di Pomino. Minimum 10 visitors, maximum 20.

PONTASSIEVE
Chianti Ruffino Via Aretina 42/44. Tel: 055 8302307 (Signor Righi). All year except Aug and Christmas. T. E. G. Fr. TP. Small wine museum.

Fattoria Bossi Via dello Stracchino 32. Tel: 055 8317830 (Bernardo Gondi). All year. T. E. Fr. TP. WS. Audio-visual presentation.

Fattoria Selvapiana Via Selvapiana 3. Tel: 055 8304848 (Francesco Giuntini, Franco Masseti). All year. T. E. G. Fr. TF. WS. Museum and ancient villa.

Florence has the headquarters of two of Tuscany's most famous producers, Antinori and Frescobaldi, and of the Consorzio del Gallo Nero, the organization with the symbol of the black cockerel which promotes Chianti Classico. The imposing Palazzo Antinori (in Piazza Antinori, on all the maps) has a wine bar in its courtyard which is well worth visiting. The Chianti Classico Consorzio also has a shop for a range of its wines, together with suitable foods, in the centre of Florence.

Chianti: Florence red

The Napoleonic Wars created a boom in what was known then in England as Florence wine, the wine that developed into Chianti.

Chianti became a great succcess simply because of the invention in the 19th century of one Laborel Melini (whose company are still one of the leading Chianti producers), who devised a strengthened wicker-based *fiasco* or covering, thereby making it possible to cork the flasks properly. Its grape composition was the product of the research of Italy's second Prime Minister, Bettino Ricasoli, another famous name whose estate is still one of the largest producers.

D.O.C. status was granted in 1967, and the more rigorous D.O.C.G. classification was just in time in 1984 to save the name of Chianti, which was almost terminally associated with a sea of cheap, mass-produced and discredited wine. Fortunately, Chianti is now more reliable and respected than ever.

Chianti types

There are two types of Chianti. The first is meant to be drunk within a year of production and is a light red and sometimes slightly *pétillant* wine with a slightly bitter bite to it. This is the 'pasta wine'. The second, Chianti Riserva, is an altogether more serious wine for laying down and ageing. Produced on the estates of Tuscan Castelli, Ville, and Fattorie, it is Italy's equivalent to the Bordeaux Château style of wine.

Chianti comes from all over Tuscany, not just the Classico area south of Florence. In general, Chianti Classico makes better Riserva wine, while Chianti from outside that area makes excellent quaffing wine. With Chianti Classico fetching twice the price of other Chiantis, there are some very good-value everyday Chiantis to be enjoyed in Tuscany.

Wine roads east of Florence

Several Chianti companies have their headquarters at Pontassieve, east of Florence on the SS67. Here you will find Chianti Ruffino. Try their white Cabreo wine for something white and sophisticated, or Chianti Classico Aziano for a textbook Chianti.

A few kilometres further east is Pomino, one of the four classic wine growing areas delimited by Cosimo de' Medici's proclamation of 1716. Frescobaldi have an estate here and are famous for their oak-aged white Pomino, called Il Benefizio, a buttery wine not unlike a white Burgundy. Frescobaldi wines come from their estates in this area which is also the area of Chianti Rùfina. Their Castello di Nipozzano estate nearby can be visited and has a small wine museum in a twelfth-century castle.

Frescobaldi's Castello di Nipozzano offers a panoramic view of the Chianti Rùfina district, one of the seven Chianti-producing areas of Tuscany. It also contains a wine museum.

San Gimignano

COLLE VAL D'ELSA
Cantina della Fortuna
Piazza S. Caterina, Colle
Alta. Tel: 0577 923102. TP.
WS.

PECCIOLI
Cantina Pasqualetti Gino
Via Risorgimento 50. Tel:
0587 635321. All week
0800–1930. Cantina with
Enoteca.

**S. CASCIANO VAL DI
PESA**
**Antica Fattoria Niccolò
Machiavelli** 50026 S.
Andrea in Percussina. Tel:
055 820027 (Nunzio
Capurso). All year except
Aug. T. E. G. TF. WS.
Machiavelli museum.

S. GIMIGNANO
The town of San
Gimignano is full of wine
and food gift shops.
**Casa Vinicola e Enoteca
Bruni** Via Quercecchio
61, Tel: 0577 940442
(Luciano Bruni). March to
mid-Nov. T (for over 15).
E. TF. WS.
Poderi Montenidoli Loc.
Montenidoli. Tel: 0577
941565 (Elisabetta
Fagiuoli). All year. T. E. G.
Fr. Sp. TF. WS.

**TAVERNELLE VAL DI
PESA**
Fattoria Poggio Romita
Via Commenda 10. Tel:
055 8077253 (Andrea
Sestini). All year. TP. WS.

An attractive route out of Pisa is to take the SS67 east to Pontedera and then to cut south towards the hilltop town San Gimignano.

After Peccioli the first city of note is Volterra, an ancient city with Etruscan walls. The wines produced in the surrounding hills are the white Bianco di S. Torpé and the red Chianti Colline Pisane.

San Gimignano's towers

The first glimpse of San Gimignano's towers is always an exciting moment as you approach the city through the undulating countryside. Too many visitors, too many gift shops and too much summer heat can make the experience unpleasant, but it's easy to see why the mediaeval buildings have become so beloved. The tall towers of the town's feuding families, the narrow mediaeval streets and courtyards, and the Palazzo del Popolo where Dante addressed the town council in 1300 (persuading them to change sides in the interminable wars between Siena and Florence) are very romantic. You can even eat in the Ristorante La Stella, where the heroine of E.M. Forster's *Room with a View* stayed, in Via San Matteo.

San Gimignano's wines

Vernaccia di San Gimignano was the first wine to be incorporated into the D.O.C. system, but its fame may owe more to the city's famous towers, which appear on its label, than to its intrinsic merit.

Vernaccia used to be made as a slightly oxidized wine that was deliberately allowed to become yellow and soupy in order to bring out the flavours of the Vernaccia grape. Few people want wine like that any more, but the danger is that cold-temperature fermentation and all the technology of modern wine-making will render the wine anonymous, just another crisp white with no particular character. To combat this, some producers are

experimenting with *barriques* to give
Vernaccia a buttery, oaky taste, while
others have produced successful
sparkling wines.

One of the best producers is
Elisabetta Fagiuoli of Montenidoli.
Her Vernaccia has exceptional
fruitiness, in fact all her wines are
organically produced and of a very
high quality. Try also Teruzzi &
Puthod's Vernaccia and Falchini's
metodo champenois Vernaccia if you
find them.

Machiavelli's wine

From San Gimignano you can either
go south-east to Siena, perhaps via
the walled town of Monteriggioni, or
north-east towards Florence via
Boccaccio's birthplace in Certaldo,
and thence into the tip of Chianti
Classico country which lies west of
the road from Florence to Siena.

The principal town here is San
Casciano Val di Pesa; it has a
modern feel to it but has notable
treasures in the Ghirlandaio
Annunciation in the Collegiata and
Santa Maria del Prato.

Two wineries are nearby. Antinori,
and just to the north, the Serristori
estate. Besides being a winery which
produces excellent Chianti Classico,
Serristori also has a small museum of
Machiavelliana in the Albergaccio
where Machiavelli lived while in exile
from Florence, and planned his great
political treatise, *The Prince*. The
nearby Tavernetta Serristori traces
its history back to the 16th century
and still functions as a tavern every
day.

*The mediaeval towers of San
Gimignano keep watch over the
Vernaccia vineyards.*

Chianti Classico

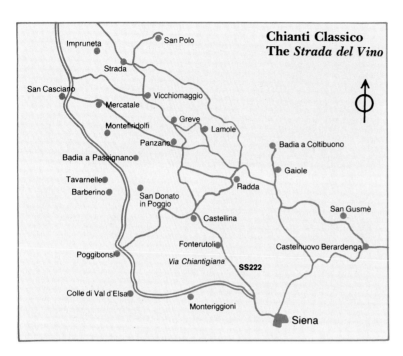

**Chianti Classico
The *Strada del Vino***

Impruneta
San Polo
Strada
San Casciano
Vicchiomaggio
Mercatale
Greve
Montefridolfi
Lamole
Panzano
Badia a Coltibuono
Badia a Passignano
Gaiole
Tavarnelle
Radda
Barberino
San Donato
in Poggio
San Gusmè
Castellina
Fonterutoli
Castelnuovo Berardenga
Poggibonsi
Via Chiantigiana SS222
Colle di Val d'Elsa
Monteriggioni
Siena

treasures, and charming villages, many unspoilt, some newly restored and revitalized by the wine trade. And most of the best known wine producers are happy to welcome visitors and to sell them wine. Not all, however, can be counted on to show visitors their winery and to give tastings. Some of the old estates have self-catering apartments, and will prepare meals for small groups of visitors if given a few days' notice (see Agriturismo, pages 98–99).

BARBERINO VAL D'ELSA
Fattoria Isole e Olena Via Olena, Loc. Isole. Tel: 055 8072763 (Paolo de Marchi). Weekdays 0800–1200, 1400–1800. Closed weekends. E. Fr. TF. WS.
Fattoria Monsanto Loc. Monsanto 16. Tel: 055 8075131 (Antonio Biliotti). Weekdays 0900–1200, 1500–1800. T. TP. WS.
Fattoria la Ripa San Donato in Poggio. Tel: 055 8072948 (Sandro Caramelli). All year. t. E. Fr. TP. WS.

GREVE IN CHIANTI
Castello di Uzzano Via Uzzano 5. Tel: 055 854032. All year. T. E. Fr. G. TP. WS. Includes garden visit.
Fattoria del Castello di Verrazzano Loc. Castello di Verrazzano. Tel: 055 854243 (Luigi Cappellini). Apr-Oct. Weekdays 0900–1800. T. E. G. Fr. TP. WS.

Traditionally, the vines of the Chianti countryside were trained to trees that were planted around the edges of cornfields; and large tracts of the Chianti territory were covered with forest. The old face of the countryside is attractively recorded in paintings by local artists, notably the frescoes painted by Pintoricchio in the late 15th century, in the Piccolomini library, Siena Cathedral. Now, as elsewhere, the vines are trained in regimented rows, and the land is dotted with cypresses and olive trees.

Chianti Classico country
Chianti Classico is only one of seven recognized Chianti regions, but it is the most famous, and it is strictly controlled by the Gallo Nero Chianti Classico Consorzio.

Visiting this area is a particular pleasure, not only for the landscape and the wines, but for the range and the density of ancient monuments, small cities packed with historic

The best way to approach this area is to take the dual carriageway from Florence to Siena, and then branch off east into the winding roads of the Chianti hills. The more leisurely approach is to follow the Via Chiantigiana and let it lead you through the wine towns of the area, most of which are on the route.

There is a *Strada del Chianti Classico*, but its signs merely point out the general area in which Chianti Classico is made.

Impruneta is just on the edge of Chianti Classico land. It holds a jolly grape harvesting festival every autumn. As you drive out of Impruneta in the Greve direction you suddenly arrive in Chianti Classico land, *Siete nel mondo del Chianti Classico*, as the big roadside signs proclaim.

At Ponte di Gabbiano visit Castelli del Grevepesa co-operative. Their single-vineyard Chiantis, the Panzano and Lamole, are serious wines.

Tenuta di Vicchiomaggio
Tel: 055 854079. T. E. TP. WS. Holiday apartments.

MERCATALE VAL DI PESA
Castelli del Grevepesa
Via Grevigiana 34. P.O. Box 2. Tel: 055 821101 All year Mon-Sat 0830–1200, 1400–1730. Closed Aug. T. E. G. Fr. TP. WS.

Chianti Classico vineyards are some of Tuscany's finest and most fertile.

CASTELNUOVO BERARDENGA
Az. Agr. Fattoria Pagliarese. Tel: 0577 359070 (Chiara and Antonio Sanguineti). All year. t. E. G. Fr. Sp. TP. WS. Holiday apartments.
Az. Agr. S. Felice Loc. S. Felice. Tel: 0577 359087 (Laura Lorenzini). Mon-Fri 0830–1030, 1330–1730. T. TP. WS.
Fattoria di Felsina Strada Chiantigiana 484. Tel: 0577 355117 (Marcello Miglioli). Mon-Fri 0900–1200, 1430–1730, Sat 0900–1230. t. TP. WS.

PANZANO
Fattoria Montagliari Via Montagliari 28. Tel: 055 852014 (Signor Giovanni Cappelli). All year. T. E. TP. WS.

GAIOLE IN CHIANTI
Agricoltori Chianti Geografico Via Mulinaccio 10. Tel: 0577 749489 (Fausto Poli). All year. t. E. Fr. TF. WS.
Az. Agr. Capannelle Capannelle. Tel: 0577 749691 (Raffaele Rossetti). All year except Jan. T. E. TF. WS.
Az. Agr. Castello di S. Polo in Rosso Loc. S. Polo in Rosso. Tel: 0577 746046 (Cesare and Katrina Canessa). Castle. WS in estate shop at Lecche.
Casa Vinicola Barone Ricasoli Cantine di Brolio. Tel: 0577 749710 (Maria Douglas). All year. T (for groups). E. Fr. Sp. TP. WS.
Riecine Loc. Riecine. Tel: 0577 749527 (John and Palmina Abbagnano Dunkley). Apr 1– Nov 30. T. TP. WS. 2–16 visitors.

Chianti castles
Further on towards Greve are three castle estates, all noteworthy: Castello di Uzzano is a historic site, a castle that successfully defied the Medici forces; Castello di Verrazzano, birthplace of the discoverer of New York Bay, Giorgio di Verrazzano; and Castello di Vicchiomaggio, now owned by an English wine producer. All three of these estates produce wine and will give tastings at a few days' notice. Vicchiomaggio, besides its excellent Chianti, also offers accommodation in the castle. West of Greve is the Badia a Passignano, with frescoes by the Florentine painter Ghirlandaio, a great recorder of Florentine life in the 15th century, and others. The monastery is now a villa, with a restaurant attached.

Greve to Panzano
Greve is a market town that benefited greatly from the peaceful years that followed the end of centuries of Florentine/Sienese feuding. This is

the capital of the wine country, where the most important Chianti Classico fair is held every September. There are three specialized wine shops.

Still on the Via Chiantigiana, Panzano has a specialist wine shop, the Enoteca del Chianti Classico.

Turning west towards Barberino Val d'Elsa, there are two contrasting estates on the way from San Donato in Poggio to Poggibonsi along a very winding road: Isole e Olena produces modern, fruity, delicious Chianti that has attracted much notice abroad; Monsanto produces expensive Chianti that is complex, spicy, and intended for long ageing.

Panzano to Radda
Radda is a mediaeval town with an economy mainly based on wine. Fattoria Vignale here is a wine-producing estate with a hotel, and attached to it a historical institute for students of Chianti history.

Nearby are two estates with typical Chianti histories. Volpaia is a mediaeval village still with its donjon or fort, recently restored by its Milanese owners. They have breathed new life into the small decaying village, and now there is an art exhibition every summer in the local church, and the wine from the estate has gained an excellent reputation.

Neighbouring Montevertine produces the upmarket table wines, Le Pergole Torte and Il Sodaccio. These wines are serious wines, something to draw the connoisseur. You can also visit the small wine museum in the Montevertine cellars.

Castellina and nearby
Castellina in Chianti was an important fortified border town (as its

name implies) in the struggles between Florence and Siena. The Bottega del Vino Gallo Nero in the town also sells the excellent local olive oil.

Castellina has a summer festival, the Estate Castellinese, on weekends in August. Stalls are set up to sell gastronomic specialities and there is dancing in the main piazza.

Vineyards surround the ruins of the Monastery of San Niccolo just outside the town towards Poggibonsi, where the Castellare estate makes organic wines. They also sell Grappa and olive oil.

Laborel Melini's estate

Further towards Poggibonsi is the Melini estate, originally the vineyards of the celebrated Laborel Melini (see also page 84), who invented the strengthened Chianti *fiasco* and also the process of heat-treating wine to ensure its stability and hence transportability.

Now the estate belongs to the huge modern conglomerate of Italian wine companies, the Gruppo Italiano Vini; their normal Chianti is a sound commercial wine, but their single-vineyard wines are of outstandingly high quality.

Castello di Brolio is the home of the illustrious Ricasoli family, which has included both statesmen and wine-producers (see page 92).

GAIOLE IN CHIANTI (Cont)

Tenuta di Coltibuono
Loc. Badia a Coltibuono. Tel: 0577 759498 (Jon McInnes). All year. T. E. TP. WS. Minimum 10 visitors. 11th-century monastery, cellars, gardens, wine shop, oil tastings.

The Gallo Nero (black cockerel)

This emblem of the Chianti Classico Consorzio, a familiar neck label on their members' bottles, was the symbol of the mediaeval Chianti League.

It recalls the meeting of two knights who were to have ridden out from Siena and Florence exactly at cockcrow, towards each other, along the Via Chiantigiana. Their meeting point was supposed to establish the future boundary between the warring cities.

The black cockerel of Florence, scrawny and underfed, woke his rider up much earlier than the pampered Sienese cockerel. And consequently the riders met at Fonterutoli, much nearer Siena than Florence.

LECCHI DI GAIOLE IN CHIANTI

Fattoria di Ama Ama in Chianti. Tel: 0577 746031 (Silvano Formigli). All year. T. TP. WS.

RADDA IN CHIANTI

Fattoria Castello di Volpaia Volpaia. Tel: 0577 738066 (Giovanella Stianti). All year. T. E. Fr. TP. WS. Minimum 6 visitors.

Fattoria di Monte Vertine Tel: 0577 738009 (Klaus Johann Reimitz). All year. t. E. G. TP. WS.

Relais Fattoria Vignale Via Pianigiani 15. Tel: 0577 738012. Small hotel and wine estate. TP. WS.

Gaiole

The *comune* of Gaiole is in the south-eastern corner of Chianti Classico. It is predominantly hilly and an area much fought over in mediaeval times. An interesting route to take is the *Strada dei Castelli del Chianti*, which is clearly marked with a castle and grape logo. Castles, abbeys, churches and views are pointed out.

Beyond Gaiole, where you should visit the Co-operative Agricoltori del Chianti Geografico and the Enoteca Montagnani wine shop, the road leads to two exceptional estates.

Riecine is where John Dunkley, a former London businessman, makes a carefully crafted and ultra-traditional Chianti Classico.

Neighbouring Badia a Coltibuono is an imposing monument in its own right. The abbey church is one of the outstanding mediaeval legacies in the Chianti region. The monastery is now privately owned, and may not be visited. But fortunately there is an *osteria* just down the hill where you can buy the splendid products of this estate: olive oil and Chianti.

Gaiole to Castelnuovo Berardenga

As you leave Gaiole, heading southwards, or alternatively if you have come from Radda, visit Castello di Ama and San Polo in Rosso as a diversion on the way south.

The lover of wine history, and those who are interested in improbable architecture, will also want to stop at the astonishing Castello di Brolio. This palatial 19th-century pile, built in the Neogothic style, is the stronghold of the celebrated Ricasoli family; it was built by Baron Bettino Ricasoli who created in the 1830s the classic Chianti grape mix that is still used

today. He also became the second Prime Minister of united Italy. The view from the ramparts of Castello di Brolio is a wonderful panorama of the tranquil, Chianti countryside, well worth the visit.

Not far from Brolio, there are three more estates worth visiting: San Felice (besides the Chianti Classico, try the Vigorello and Poggio Rosso); Pagliarese, where the Fattoria is built on the ruins of a 13th-century fort (try the Riserva Chianti Classico); and Giuseppe Mazzocolin's Fattoria di Felsina just outside Castelnuovo (taste the Chianti Classico and a *barrique*-aged upmarket table wine called Fontalloro).

Siena versus Florence

Siena is sometimes overlooked in favour of its more cosmopolitan rival, Florence, indeed the two cities have been rivals for many hundreds of years, and for much of the Middle Ages they were actually at war, a struggle eventually won by Florence.

The conflict has left its mark upon the present day. Sienese residents do not go to Florence if they can help it – and vice versa with Florentines.

Perhaps it is a sense of being in the shadow of Florence that prompts the Sienese to do so much for the winemakers of the province. Certainly Siena leads the way in the publication of helpful brochures for the wine tourist (see pages 98–99).

In fact, Siena has much to offer. Besides being the home of the *Palio* (the horserace run on the piazza beneath the towering mediaeval Palazzo Pubblico) and perhaps the most beautiful cathedral in Italy, it is also the home of Italy's Permanent National Wine Exhibition, the *Enoteca Permanente*.

Siena: the Enoteca Permanente

The Enoteca is sited in the east bastion of the great fortress built by Cosimo I, Grand Duke of Tuscany, on the edge of the town. The castle was originally built by the Medici Duke as a defence against his old enemy, the Sienese people.

The wide, spiralling munitions staircase leads to the vaults where a selected 600 best Italian wines are displayed. In the upper rooms and terraces the visitor has a marvellous opportunity to taste and discuss wines from all over Italy with the knowledgeable staff. Ask for the Wine List; it's a comprehensive beginner's guide to Italian wines.

GAGGIANO POGGIBONSI
Melini
Tel: 0577 939667 (Nunzio Capurso). All year except Aug. T. E. G. TF. WS.

SIENA
Permanent Italian Wine Exhibition Fortezza Medicea. Tel: 0577 288497. Daily 1500–2400. TP. WS. Information on all Italian wines.

One of Siena's glories is its Enoteca (left), Italy's only national wine centre, and an ideal place to taste the fine wines of Siena. The huge late-mediaeval cathedral (below) is another attraction.

Montalcino

South of Siena the countryside changes dramatically. The hills of Chianti with their olive trees, vines and woods give way to the hills of Le Crete Senesi, a beautiful area to travel through, especially before the harvest when the cornfields and sunflowers gild the hills with different shades of yellow, giving the few clumps of cypresses in their midst an almost surreal air.

The SS2 from Siena is part of the old Pilgrims Way to Rome, the Via Francigena. This particular stretch is called the Via Cassia.

Buonconvento is the first town of note along the route. Its 14th-century walls are still in good repair. A yellow tourist sign signals the turning to the Abbey of Monte Oliveto Maggiore, where the frescoes by Sodoma and Signorelli make the detour worthwhile.

The town of Montalcino

When you have arrived it's best to abandon the car and walk everywhere. There are two indispensable stops in this town: the first is the Wine Exhibition Centre in the offices of the Consorzio for , Brunello, where they will also be happy to give you further information as required. (The symbol of the Consorzio is the holm oak; Montalcino derives its name from the oak trees recorded in its Latin name: Mons Ilcinis.)

The second is the Enoteca/wine bar in the castle of Montalcino. The castle was the last fortress of the Sienese Republic to hold out against the Florentines. Conquered in 1559, some four centuries passed before the town erected a plaque in the fortress to record the shame of the 'Medici Robbers'.

The great Brunello

The credit for the invention of Brunello goes to the ancestor of its most famous producers: the Biondi Santi family. It was Clemente Santi who created Brunello in the 1850s and it is Franco Biondi Santi and his son Jacopo who continue the tradition today. Their wines are fabulously long-lived, and fabulously expensive too.

Not all producers succeed in making wines that last as long. Casanova dei Neri, for example, make wines that can be drunk within six years or so of the vintage. As with Barolo, changing tastes and changing economics have forced a change in wine style.

A development of the public demand for younger, fruitier reds, and the producers' need to sell wines as early as possible has been the creation of a younger cousin of Brunello di Montalcino called simply Rosso di Montalcino. It's a very attractive fruity wine of some finesse despite its youth.

Books and fine wine

Brunello producers claim that their wine is the finest that Italy can offer. The wine has great prestige in the United States; the British like it too.

The story goes that former British Prime Minister Harold Macmillan was entertaining the publisher Mondadori and another Italian at 10 Downing Street. The conversation turned to wine, and they considered which were the finest wines of all. The Italians suggested French classics, Gevrey Chambertin and Montrachet. Macmillan said he was surprised they hadn't heard of Brunello di Montalcino; perhaps they would like to try some of his

MONTALCINO
Enoteca La Fortezza. Tel: 0577 849211. Summer 0900–1300, 1400–2000, winter 0900–1300, 1400–1800. Closed Mon. TP. WS. Inside the castle of Montalcino.
Antico Podere Canneta. Tel: 0577 848692 (Angelo Clerico). All year. T. E. TF. WS.
Az. Agr. Altesino. Loc. Altesino. Tel: 0577 806208. All year. T. E. G. WS.
Az. Agr. Casanova dei Neri Podere Casanova, Torrenieri. Tel: 0577 834029 (Giacomo Neri). All year. E. Fr. TF. WS.
Az. Agr. Pacenti Franco Canalicchio. Tel: 0577 849277 (Carla Pacenti). All year. T. TF. WS.
Fattoria dei Barbi e del Casato Taverna, Norcineria, Caseificio. Tel: 0577 848277 (Angela Marconi). All year. T (for groups). E. TF. WS. Historic cellars with Vin Santo going back to 1870. Holiday apartments.
Tenuta Caparzo Loc. Torrenieri. Tel: 0577 848390 (Marina Bracalente). Jan-Dec. T. TF. WS. Minimum 5 visitors.

favourite Brunello from the Barbi Colombini estate?

The proof is in the tasting; the Fattoria dei Barbi is well worth visiting. It makes and sells its wine, and also produces its own salami and cheese. It has a restaurant where these products are served, and you can visit the historic cellars.

The prospect of making money out of something as congenial as wine has encouraged development in Montalcino, and increasingly high prices. The biggest development has been the buying up of vineyards by outsiders, many of them Milanese.

The most important of these outsiders, however, is the American-owned Villa Banfi, which made its fortune from Lambrusco. Villa Banfi has injected millions of dollars into Montalcino and literally moved whole hillsides to produce the optimum vineyard sites. Their Brunello is a very accessible wine; look out also for their Moscadello, a sweet wine that Montalcino used to be famous for before Brunello was invented. It has been re-invented by Villa Banfi in response to the new demand for light, slightly sparkling white wines.

The logo of the Consorzio of Brunello (above) bears the symbol of Montalcino, the leaves of the holm oak. The countryside around Montalcino (below) is wooded and hilly, with sunflowers in the valley and vineyards on the hillsides.

Montepulciano

About half an hour's drive east from Montalcino is its great rival, Montepulciano, the zone of the splendidly named Vino Nobile. To reach it you drive through some of the prettiest countryside in Tuscany.

Renaissance Pienza

An absolute must is a visit to the charming miniature town of Pienza, which had the great good fortune to be the birthplace of Aeneas Silvio Piccolomini, Pope Pius II, and was largely rebuilt by him in a few years, from 1459. The town became his new summer residence, and following

papal example, bishops and nobles began building themselves palaces here too. Then, after Piccolomini died in 1464, building stopped, and since then the town has largely been undisturbed. Visit the Palazzo Piccolomini in the courtyard-like main piazza.

Vino Nobile

The first wine to be granted D.O.C.G. status was Vino Nobile di Montepulciano. It is Brunello's rival, and has the commercial advantage of being ready to drink sooner because of its fewer years of ageing. Like Brunello it also has a younger version, Rosso di Montepulciano. In general it's a very accessible wine well adapted to the modern taste with a strong fruity character without being excessively tannic or bitter. Buy some now, before its impending popularity drives the prices up.

Renaissance Montepulciano

It is about 14km (9 miles) to the hill town of Montepulciano from Pienza. The first feature you see is the Renaissance church of S. Biagio, halfway up the slope. The whole town is something of an architect's dream. Sangallo the Elder was responsible for much of it, in the early 16th century, and the town is certainly as *nobile* as the Montepulciano wine; it is full of beautiful Renaissance palaces.

Discovering wines brings many opportunities for architectural exploration; or vice-versa maybe. Entering Montepulciano by the Porta al Prato, the first little square you encounter has a statue of Il Marzocco, the Florentine lion, demonstrating the city's allegiance to the Medici.

The heraldic griffin, which gives its name to the Grifi wine (right), is also the symbol on the logo of the Consorzio of Vino Nobile producers (below).

Palazzo Avignonesi

Just opposite the lion is the lovely Palazzo Avignonesi; it's in all the guidebooks. Its wine is not cheap, but it is some of the best that can be found in Tuscany. You can taste the Vino Nobile, the Grifi and the various whites, including an excellent Chardonnay, in the reception rooms of the palazzo.

The prettiest piazza

Following the street from the palazzo up into the town there is a constant succession of delightful buildings, reaching a climax with a piazza that could claim to be the prettiest in all Italy. The Palazzo Comunale is a miniature version of Florence's Palazzo Vecchio, and the cathedral and *palazzi* that form the other three sides of the square are like something out of a cardboard stage set; they are a perfectly designed ensemble.

One of the piazza's many perfectly-staged *palazzi* is the Palazzo Contucci; this is another good wine excuse, for Alamanno Contucci is President of the Vino Nobile Consorzio, and a noted producer himself. A small shop sells his wine in the palazzo.

GRACCIANO DI MONTEPULCIANO
Az. Agr. Poliziano Via Fontago 1. Tel: 0578 738171 (Dr Carletti). All year except Aug and Christmas. T (for groups). E. TF. WS.

MONTEPULCIANO
Montepulciano has many wine shops, principally in Via Gracciano del Corso and in the main piazza. Most sell only the wine of their owners. TP. WS. **Avignonesi snc** Via Gracciano del Corso 91. Tel: 0578 757874. All year. t. E. Fr. TF. WS. Historic cellars in 16th-century palazzo.

S. ANGELO IN COLLE
Az. Lisini. Tel: 0577 864040 (Lorenzo Lisini Baldi). All year. T. E. Fr. TP. WS. 17th-century villa (9km/6 miles from Montalcino).

SINALUNGA
Fassati Casa Vinicola del Chianti Via Grosseto 18. (Offices: Via XX Settembre 98g, 00187 Roma). Tel: 06 4741041 (Michele Miglietta). Feb–Jul, Sept–Nov. T (2 weeks in advance). E. Fr. TP. WS.

Palazzo Contucci is one of Montepulciano's many beautiful buildings, a classic example of the Renaissance town palace of a noble family.

Food and Festivals

FURTHER INFORMATION

Associazione Nazionale per l'Agriturismo Corso Vittorio Emanuele 101, Rome.

Consorzio Colline Lucchesi Viale Marsanti/Matteucci, 55100 Lucca. Tel: 0583 43061.

Consorzio del Chianti Putto Lungarno Corsini 4, 50123 Firenze. Tel: 055 212333/210168.

Consorzio del Gallo Nero Via de'Serragli 146, 50124 Firenze. Tel: 055 229351.

Consorzio Vini di Montalcino Costa del Municipio 1, 53024 Montalcino. Tel: 0577 848246.

Consorzio del Vino Montecarlo Palazzo Agricoltura, Borgo Gianotti, 55100 Lucca.

Consorzio del Vino Nobile di Montepulciano Via delle Case Nuove 15, 53045 Montepulciano. Tel: 0578 757844.

Ente Provinciale per il Turismo di Firenze Via A. Manzoni 16, 50121 Firenze. Tel: 055 2478141.

Ente Provinciale per il Turismo di Siena Via de Città 5, 53100 Siena. Tel: 0577 47051. The brochure *Strada dei Castelli del Chianti* available here gives detailed itineraries for visiting the Gaiole area and discovering castles, abbeys, churches and wineries.

FOOD SPECIALITIES

Until the quality of the ingredients is appreciated, Tuscan food can seem severe and parsimonious. This is, perhaps, the reason for the fame of *Bistecca alla fiorentina*, a generous rib steak, an island in the sea of soups and beans.

But as good members of this nation of food critics, the Tuscans are fascinated by their food, and their preoccupation is above all with the quality of the raw ingredients. When the wine estate of Castello della Sala was officially opened to the world's press a few years ago, what really excited the prestigious Antinori company was that they could serve a meal composed of meat, fruit, vegetables and wine, with all products coming from their own estate. No problems with hiring internationally renowned chefs, just the freshest ingredients simply cooked. Typically Tuscan.

Tuscany is justly famous for its simple foods. The extra-vergine olive oil is so fruity, rich and thick, it is almost a meal in itself. But it is not so plentiful or so cheap now as it was before the great frost of 1985 which destroyed so many of Chianti's abundant olive trees. New shoots have now sprung from the frost-blasted trees, but it may still be many years before olive oil production recovers fully.

Olive oil is used for cooking, but its main purpose is to bring out the flavour of cooked foods. The *Bistecca* and the *Ribollita*, bean soup that is cooked twice, 'reboiled', is delicious laced with local olive oil.

Liver is much loved here. A favourite is *Fegatelli* (or *Fegatini di maiale all'uccelletto*), a type of kebab of pig's liver, bay leaf, and traditional Tuscan unsalted bread. *Crostini di fegatini* is a dish of toasted rounds of Tuscan bread served with a delicious liver and anchovy paste.

Pasta is not a traditional Tuscan food, but it does appear in dishes

AGRITURISMO

Staying on a wine estate

In the main wine-producing areas of Italy there is now a growing demand for self-catering houses and apartments for rent, especially during the summer season.

Tuscany is particularly rich in this type of accommodation. Wine producers have converted their villa stable blocks or outlying barns into holiday homes, and some have even converted their own castles or Fattorie into hotels.

Booklets and further information

An excellent booklet on Agriturismo throughout Italy, the *Guida dell'Ospitalità Rurale*, is available from the Associazione Nazionale per l'Agriturismo in Rome.

For Tuscany in particular the booklet *Chianti: locations, culture, itineraries, wines* is very useful, covering accommodation and wine-tastings offered by members of the Chianti Classico, together with a history of the area. It is available from the Consorzio del Gallo Nero in Florence.

which combine the hunter's catch with rich sauces: *Pappardelle alla lepre*, for example, is wide pasta strips with a hare sauce.

Hunting, once common in the great forests of Tuscany, is still a favourite activity, and it can produce wild boar in various remote parts of Tuscany. But it is more likely to entail the shooting of *conigli* – rabbits, or *uccelletti* – small birds, which are cooked on a spit and eaten bones and all.

The Tuscan coast provides several fish specialities: *Triglie alla livornese* is red mullet cooked with tomatoes, garlic and ginger. *Cèe* or *Cieche alla pisana* are eel fry cooked with olive oil, garlic and sage and served with parmesan. Salt cod, *Baccalà* is a speciality of Livorno, and is cooked with tomatoes and potatoes.

Finocchio – fennel, is baked with butter and parmesan as an accompaniment to roast meats, and is used to great effect to flavour a special type of salami, the *finocchiona*.

Details of accommodation and wine-tastings on wine estates in the province of Siena are provided in two booklets, *Turismo nel Chianti* and *In Vacanza con Noi*. General information on holiday homes in southern Tuscany is covered in *Vacanze in Campagna*, all available from the Ente Provinciale per il Turismo di Siena. For detailed itineraries in the Gaiole area, and more information on its castles, abbeys and churches, consult the *Strada dei Castelli del Chianti* brochure, also from the Siena tourist office.

FESTIVALS

February: VIAREGGIO : one of the most famous carnivals of Italy.
April: FLORENCE: Easter festival, the 'Explosion of the Cart'. The singing of the Gloria in the Duomo sets off a firework explosion.
May: PONTASSIEVE: Toscanello d'Oro, an exhibition of Chianti wine.
May or June: FLORENCE: Firenze a Tavola exhibition, Fortezza da Basso, an internationally famous annual food and wine fair.
June: MONTESPERTOLI: Mostra Mercato del Vino Chianti.
June: FLORENCE: Historic costume 'soccer' match and parade.
June: PISA: Regatta of the Maritime Republics.
July: PISTOIA: Joust of the Bear, a costume festival.
July and August: SIENA: the Palio, the most famous city horserace in Italy.
August, last Sunday: MONTEPULCIANO: Bravìo delle Botti, a costume parade followed by wine-barrel race.
September: LUCCA: the Palio of the Terzania, a costume parade and crossbow tournament.
September, first week: MONTECARLO: Mostra Mercato deï Vini Lucchesi, Piazza d'Armi.
September, second half: LUCCA: Mostra dei Prodotti Tipici, wine, oil and honey, held in the Loggia del Palazzo Pretorio.
September: GREVE IN CHIANTI: Mostra Mercato del Vino Chianti Classico, the most important event in the Chianti showing calendar.
September: AREZZO: Joust of the Saracen, a costume tournament.
December: PRATOMAGNO: Mostra dell'Olio Extra-Vergine.

Central Italy

T he tourist brochures and guidebooks are full of the phrase *L'Italia ha un cuore verde* (Italy has a green heart), but it's true nevertheless that Umbria as a region is a gentle, green and pleasant land, with enchanting landscapes of green hills and dense forests, and some of the country's most beautiful towns. The smokestacks of industry are confined to the city of Terni. With this exception, Umbria is a jewel of the Middle Ages: Gúbbio is the archetypal mediaeval town; Perugia is a magnificent fortress on a hill; Orvieto's cathedral is one of the wonders of Italy; Spoleto is more cosmopolitan but just as antique. And Assisi needs no comment, except perhaps that even if St Francis had not inspired its immense basilica it would still be worth visiting for its hillside setting. Both historically and vinously there is an overlap with the Lazio region, where the cities of Bolsena and Viterbo share an Etruscan heritage with Umbria.

For wine lovers there are three areas of interest: Orvieto, Torgiano, and Montefalco.

Everyone has heard of Orvieto, famous for its wine and artistic treasures. Indeed Orvieto wine labels are often distinguished by a picture of the facade of Orvieto's cathedral. This wine became popular because of proximity to Tuscany – Chianti producers sold it as their white wine.

Orvieto production extends into the northern tip of Lazio. Around Lake Bolsena they make a white wine with a curious history: Est!Est!!Est!!! is its name (see page 103).

South of Perugia, near the famous majolica-producing town of Deruta, is Torgiano. Here the Lungarotti family have established an Italian institution: Cantine Lungarotti, whose national wine competition has government authorization, and whose Rubesco wine is famous.

Just outside Foligno is the town of Montefalco, whose red wine deserves to be better known. Unique to the area is the Sagrantino grape, used to supplement the more usual Sangiovese in Rosso di Montefalco, but also vinified as a red wine in its own right. The taste has been described as reminiscent of fruits of the forest. There is also a *passito* version made with semi-dried grapes.

The Castello della Sala (not open to the public) was recently restored by Antinori, whose estates produce one of Central Italy's finest wines, Orvieto.

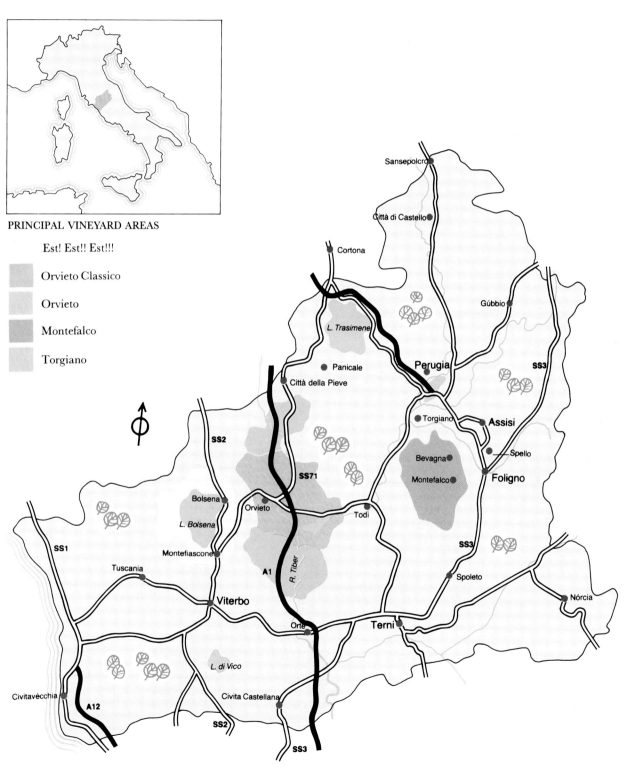

PRINCIPAL VINEYARD AREAS

Est! Est!! Est!!!

Orvieto Classico

Orvieto

Montefalco

Torgiano

Orvieto Country

The façade of the cathedral in Orvieto reflects the Italian sunshine like a gilded wedding cake. Inside there is an elaborate series of frescoes. Outside, shops in the cathedral square sell Orvieto's famous white wines.

Perugino (see his *Adoration of the Magi* in S. Maria dei Bianchi), whose most famous pupil was Raphael.

Orvieto

The sheer rock face on which Orvieto is built makes it a superb defensive site; it was much favoured by the Popes and remained part of the Papal States until 1860. As such, it remains largely intact, and the old town still fills its table-top position.

The cathedral is quite unique and though the mosaics on the facade were heavily restored in the 19th century, they follow the original design of the 14th century.

Orvieto wine

Wine-making in Orvieto goes back at least as far as the Etruscans and may even be reflected in the town's name.

One legend has barbarian invaders foiled in their attempt to carry off chalices by the metal inexplicably turning to gold. *Aurum vetitum* they shrieked, giving the city its name, and ran away. Another story, no doubt put about by wine-makers in the not too distant past, suggests that the *aurum vetitum* was none other than the golden wine that also bears the name Orvieto. It is nonetheless true that the wine, especially the sweeter *abboccato* Orvieto, does have a genuinely golden colour.

Orvieto has declined in popularity since the days when it was sold as the Chianti producers' white wine. It is certainly in danger of becoming a rather anonymous wine, as modern fermentation techniques turn it into yet another crisp, light, white with no particular character at all. But in the right hands, the dry *secco* Orvieto can be an excellent quaffing wine, while the *abboccato* version, which is rather

The easiest route to Orvieto from Tuscany is the A1 motorway, the *Autostrada del Sole.*

Various diversions are possible, notably to Chiusi for its National Etruscan Museum and to Città della Pieve, the birthplace of the artist

A view over Lake Bolsena from Grotte di Castro reveals the land of Est!Est!!Est!!!

sweeter, is refreshing without being cloying.

Contrasting producers

Just north of Orvieto, near Ficulle, is Antinori's Castello della Sala. It is not open to the public, but it's worth admiring its magnificent position.

Between La Sala and Orvieto is the Bigi company. Their *cru* Orvieto, Vigneto Torricella, is an excellent product of modern methods.

Decugnano dei Barbi lies east of Orvieto on the way to Todi. They produce Orvieto of real character and finesse, even producing a dessert Orvieto made like Sauternes.

Est!Est!!Est!!!

The other wine of note in this area lies in the zone of Montefiascone, between Bolsena and Viterbo. Est!Est!!Est!!! can be pleasant enough, but it's normally of only passing interest. The fascination lies in the origin of its Latin name with its plethora of exclamation marks.

The story behind the wine dates back to early mediaeval times. It is said that a certain German prelate, Bishop Fugger, was journeying south to Rome around the year 1000, accompanied by a servant whose task it was to travel ahead of his master to find the best inns with the best wine. Having found a suitable hostelry, the servant would write Est! on the door to indicate its suitability, and then hurry on to the next place.

On reaching Montefiascone, the servant was so struck by the quality of the local wine that he wrote not one Est! but three on the door, complete with exclamation marks. Apparently his master was equally convinced of the quality of the wine, for he died of drinking too much of it, and was buried in the same place. Until the 17th century, a barrel of wine was emptied on the bishop's grave every anniversary of his death.

CASTIGLIONE IN TEVERINA
Casa Vinicola Conte Vaselli Piazza Poggetto 12. Tel: 0761 948305. All year except Aug and Sept. Mon-Fri 1000–1200, 1500–1700. T. TP. WS.

ORVIETO
Az. Agr. Decugnano dei Barbi Loc. Fossatello di Corbara. Tel: 0763 24055 (Enrico Costanti). All year. T. WS. Maximum 12.
Barberani Az. Agr. Vallesanta Loc. Cerreto, Baschi. Tel: 0744 950113 (Dr Luigi Antonio Barberani). Weekdays. t. Fr. TF. WS. The company wine shop, **Enoteca Barberani**, is in the Piazza Duomo, Orvieto.
Casa Vinicola Luigi Bigi e Figlio Loc. Ponte Giulio. Tel: 0763 26224 (Alberto Ceripa). All year except Aug. T. E. G. TF. WS.
Tenuta le Velette Loc. Le Velette, Orvieto Stazione. Tel: 0763 29090. Apr 15–Oct 10. Closed Suns. T. TP. WS.

VITERBO
Cantina Co-op. Montefiascone Via Cassia Montefiascone. Tel: 0761 86148. T. TP. WS.
Enoteca La Torre Via della Torre 5. Tel: 0761 226467. 1700–2400. Closed Sun.

The Province of Perugia

BEVAGNA
Az. Agr. Adanti Vocabolo Arquata. Tel : 0742 360295 (Alvaro Palini, Daniela Adanti). All year. t. E. Fr. TF. WS.

Cantine Benincasa Loc. Capro 99. Tel: 0742 682307 (Domenico Benincasa). Office hours, but Sat preferred. T. TP. WS.

MONTEFALCO
Tenuta Val di Maggio Loc. Torre. Tel: 0742 79690 (Arnaldo Caprai). Weekdays 0900–1200, 1500–1800. T. TP. WS.

PANICALE
Cantina Lamborghini Loc. Soderi 1. Tel : 075 9589197. All year. T. E. TF. WS. Collection of Lamborghini cars and tractors.

The attractive hillside wine town of Montefalco, home of Rosso di Montefalco, is surrounded by its vineyards.

Umbria, the green heart of Italy, is a fertile region; but wine has never been a major component of its agriculture. The grape accounts for less than 5 per cent of its produce and precedence is given to livestock, cereals, tobacco and eggs. Most wine produced is even now still destined for home consumption.

There are two approaches to northern Umbria and the region's capital of Perugia. One way is via Città di Castello and the Tiber Valley; the D.O.C. red and white wine Colli Altotiberini comes from here but is of mainly local interest.

The other way is via Cortona and Lake Trasimene. D.O.C. Colli del Trasimeno is mainly of local interest too. More interesting is to reflect, as you pass them by, on the village names, Ossaia (ossuary) and Sanguineto (bloody), which indicate the area of Hannibal's victory in 217 BC, at the battle of Lake Trasimene.

To the south of Lake Trasimene near the town of Panicale, is the Lamborghini winery. Their wine is not in quite the same class as their cars, but it's worth tasting.

Perugia
Perugia is a great cultural centre and combines the rural simplicity of Umbria with the style of a University city. Raphael began his career in Perugia, and the painters Pintoricchio and Perugino also worked here. The Galleria Nazionale dell'Umbria, one of Italy's finest art galleries, is housed in the magnificent Palazzo dei Priori. Don't miss the Archaeological Museum and the Etruscan Tomb of the Volumnii just outside the town to the south.

For an overview, and tasting, of Umbrian wines visit the Enoteca Provinciale di Perugia, an exhibition of Perugian wines and D.O.C. Umbrian wines in vaulted cellars.

Torgiano
It is only a few kilometres south to Torgiano where the world's wine press gather every year for the Banco d'Assaggio National Wine Competition at the Lungarotti estate. Visit the impressive wine museum and have a drink at the *osteria*. A booking is necessary to visit the cellars and taste Lungarotti's excellent Torre di Giano, Cabernet Sauvignon, Chardonnay and riserva wine Rubesco (the single vineyard Vigna Monticchio is highly regarded).

Assisi and Spello
Umbria is full of exquisite mediaeval sights. Following the Topino valley south from Perugia the first stop is Assisi. It is a tourist trap, but the basilica of St Francis is wonderfully frescoed, with masterpieces of pictorial narrative by Giotto and many others. It has such atmosphere that the souvenir stalls outside fail to ruin it. And, as with all tourist traps,

The Lungarotti wine museum at Torgiano houses a rich collection of wine-related artifacts, including old wine presses and huge earthenware wine jars, collected by Maria Grazia Lungarotti, wife of the wine-maker Dr Giorgio Lungarotti.

it is enough to walk away from the main thoroughfares to escape the crowds. Climb up to the castle and peer down through the gunports at the town below you if the tourist throng gets too much for you.

Spello, some 6km (4 miles) away has everything: a Roman theatre, Roman gates, and Perugino and Pintoricchio frescoes. Every year at the feast of Corpus Christi, the streets are decorated with mosaics in ·petals and seeds.

Montefalco

I must declare a personal interest in the wine of Montefalco. My first year in Italy was spent in Foligno (between Montefalco and Spello), a town chiefly known for its railway junction and barracks where, so the conscripts said, the chief activity was cleaning the donkey stables. Foligno's grocery shops offered only 2-litre Vino Rosso or 75cl Rosso di Montefalco 1976. Having been brought up on the wines of France, I

had no idea what to expect. But I found the Rosso di Montefalco truly superb – yet no one outside the area had heard of it. The year I left, Rosso di Montefalco was made a D.O.C. wine. Totally unjustifiably, I felt that my constant praise for this wine had something to do with it.

Visit Montefalco for its frescoed churches, its town walls and its mediaeval atmosphere. Nearby Bevagna, where the Adanti family make their excellent Sagrantino (see pages 100–101), is notable for its typically Umbrian Romanesque churches.

Despite the relatively small scale of wine production in Umbria, the past few years have seen a steady increase in the number of recognized D.O.C. zones. Two further areas of white wine production await the award of D.O.C. status. From around the antique collectors' city of Todi comes Grechetto di Todi, and from around Spoleto comes Trebbiano di Spoleto.

PERUGIA
Enoteca Provinciale di Perugia Via Ulisse Rocchi 18. Tel: 075 24824. 1000–1330, 1630–2330. Closed Mon. TP. WS. ER. Exhibition and tasting of Perugian wines and D.O.C. Umbrian wines in vaulted cellars.

TODI
Az. Agr. Vagniluca Loc. Frontignano. Tel: 075 8852179. All year. T. TP. WS.

TORGIANO
Cantine Giorgio Lungarotti SpA Tel: 075 982348 (A. Lavoratori). All year Mon- Fri 0800–1300, 1500–1800. Closed Aug and Christmas holidays. T. E. G. TF. WS. Wine can be bought from Lungarotti's **Osteria del Museo** at any time. There is also a **Museo del Vino**, a hotel **'Le Tre Vaselle'**, and a craft shop **'La Spola'**.

Food and Festivals

Central Italy is proud of an inheritance of celebrated and historic wines. This sign outside a wine shop proclaims the classic regional wines. *Produzione propria means* that the wine is the shop's own, the produce of its estate.

PIZZA A TAGLIO

Hungry tourists looking for a quick snack will appreciate one Umbrian facility, the *pizza a taglio* shops which serve pizza by the wedge, freshly cooked and ready for your mid-morning stroll or pre-dinner *passeggiata*. This custom is not specifically Umbrian, but if you have come from the North the shops may not yet be familiar to you – it's difficult to find them outside the tourist areas further north. The further south you go, the more there are of them.

FESTIVALS

February : SPELLO: Festa dell'Olio e Sagra della Bruschetta – olive oil festival and tasting.

March/April: TODI: National Antiques Fair.

April: GUBBIO (and numerous other Umbrian towns and villages): Good Friday Procession.

April/May : NARNI: Giostra all'Anello, jousting.

May: ASSISI: National Antiques Fair.

May: ASSISI: Calendimaggio, a mediaeval fair.

End May: GUBBIO: Palio della Balestra, mediaeval crossbow archery.

May: GUBBIO: Festa dei Ceri race.

June: BOLSENA: Infiorata, a flower festival on Corpus Christi.

June: ORVIETO: Corpus Christi, a mediaeval procession.

June: SPELLO: Corpus Christi flower festival.

June/July: SPOLETO: Festival of Two Worlds.

July: GRADOLI: Festival of Aleatico, local wine festival.

August: CITTA DELLA PIEVE/ CASTIGLIONE DEL LAGO: Palio dei Terzieri, a mediaeval fair.

September: FOLIGNO: Giostra della Quintana, a mediaeval joust.

October/November: GUBBIO: truffle festival.

November: CITTA DI CASTELLO: truffle festival.

FOOD SPECIALITIES

There is no particular dish that characterizes Umbrian food, though the visitor from abroad may be unable to forget the sight of *uccelletti*, little birds served whole, with their beaks wide open. More important to Umbrian cuisine than the ingredients is the method of cooking them. With a simplicity and rusticity that befits the land of Saint Francis, the spit, the grill and the wood-burning oven are the traditional cooking methods:

alla brace, *alla griglia*, and *al forno di legno* are the signs to look for.

The fruity green olive oil of Umbria is delicious, and probably shares the honours with the olive oil of Lake Garda as the best in Italy. Spello, Spoleto, the Valnerina and Amerino valleys are the centres of production. Spello holds a Sagra della Bruschetta (*bruschetta* feast) which is a celebration of toasted Umbrian bread rubbed with garlic and sprinkled with extra-virgin olive oil and salt.

Cinghiale (wild boar) is often on the menu, as are *piccioni* (pigeons) and *uccelletti* (small birds eaten whole, cooked on a spit with bay leafs and chunks of bread to separate them).

The black truffle of Norcia and Spoleto is a prized ingredient, used especially to flavour omelettes. Cheese and salami, and other pork products from Norcia, are also particularly good.

Trout from the pure waters of Fonti di Clitunno, carp from Lake Trasimene, and eels and roach provide freshwater fish.

Other regional dishes include:
Cardi alla perugina: cardoons fried in batter, then cooked in the oven with a *ragù* sauce.
Palombacce all'uso di Foligno: casseroled pigeon cooked with its giblets with olives and vegetables.
Sedani di Trevi: celery baked in a tomato sauce.
Spiedi misti Spoletini: a *brace* or spit of mixed meats.
Strangozzi di Spoleto: home-made flat pasta from Spoleto.

FURTHER INFORMATION

Azienda di Promozione Turistica di Assisi Piazza del Comune 12, Assisi. Tel: 075 812450.
Consorzio Tutela Vino D.O.C. Orvieto Classico e Orvieto Corso Cavour 36, 05018 Orvieto. Tel: 0763 43790. *Andar per vigne*, a leaflet guide to visiting Orvieto wine producers, is available here.
Ente Provinciale Turismo di Viterbo Piazza dei Caduti 16, 01100 Viterbo. Tel: 0761 226161.
Regione Umbria, Ufficio Turismo Corso Vannucci 30, Perugia. Tel: 075 6961.

The Barberani wine shop in Orvieto's cathedral square displays wines of the region.

The Adriatic Coast

The eastern side of the Apennines doesn't have the same attractions for the traveller as Tuscany or the Veneto, with their obvious cultural delights. It is the motorway-loving holiday-makers who tend to stay on this coast of Italy. Scan the map and very few towns stand out immediately: Urbino, of course, is known for its Ducal Palace; Ancona, for its port; Loreto, for the Santa Casa; Bari, for its famous church of S. Nicola; and Brindisi, for its port and the ferry for Greece.

But there is much more to discover: the hill towns of the Marches, the architectural splendour of Ascoli Piceno, the National Park of Abruzzo, the archaeological museum of Chieti, Castel del Monte, the *trulli* of Alberobello and the Baroque palaces of Lecce. The people here are different; they are more relaxed and more friendly, and more insular too. The people of Abruzzo are proud of their reputation as *forti e gentili*, hard of purpose but gentle of manner, and the same attributes apply to the Marchigiani and the Pugliesi as well.

Harvest time for Verdicchio grapes in the Monte Schiavo co-operative's vineyards.

Politically and vinously the Adriatic coast is divided into three main sections: the Marches; Abruzzo/Molise; and Puglia.

The Marches are the home of the most celebrated Adriatic wine: Verdicchio. The amphora, or Lollobrigida-shaped bottle is a familiar sight on trattoria tables abroad, and this is undoubtedly the best wine to drink with the local fish. Less well known, but perhaps to the connoisseur more interesting, are the two reds of the Marches, Rosso Conero and Rosso Piceno. Other wines of the area are of local interest only. Some producers are making excellent sparkling wines with Verdicchio grapes, and while these are too expensive to compete with other sparkling wines abroad they are very pleasant to taste during travels in the region.

In Abruzzo there are only three wines: two Montepulciano d'Abruzzos, the red, and the

Cerasuolo (rosé), and Trebbiano d'Abruzzo (white). The rosé and the white can be good, but the red is the most interesting; it's a very drinkable wine that is smooth enough even for those who find most Italian reds somewhat bitter. Molise has two wines almost impossible to find outside the region: Biferno and Pentro. They mirror the wines of Abruzzo in their dependence on the Montepulciano grape for the red and rosé, and on Trebbiano for the white wines.

Puglia is one of Italy's big four regional producers of wine, in quantity that is. The Veneto produces about as much: think of all the Soave and Valpolicella. Emilia Romagna produces slightly more (all that Lambrusco). And Sicily produces slightly more: Corvo, and a few other quality wines, as well as E.E.C. subsidies. But where does all of Puglia's wine go? The answer is only partly the E.E.C. Most of Puglia's wine is used either as the base wine for Vermouth by the Piedmontese Vermouth manufacturers or as 'cutting' wine for other Italian or foreign wines. Slowly, quality wines are emerging from this anonymous production as local pride, modern technology and demand dictate. There are 19 D.O.C. wines: the ones most commonly found are Castel del Monte, Locorotondo, Martina Franca, and Salice Salentino. Five Roses is a branded rose.

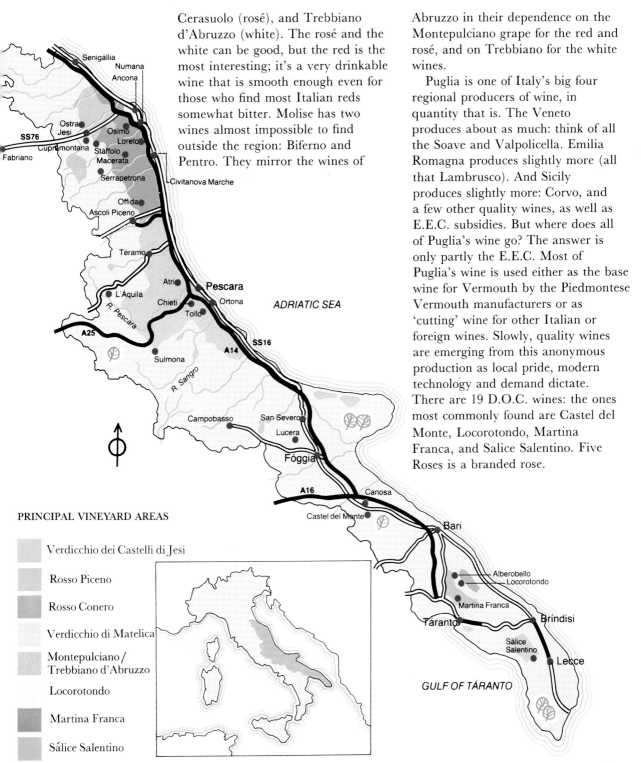

PRINCIPAL VINEYARD AREAS

Verdicchio dei Castelli di Jesi

Rosso Piceno

Rosso Conero

Verdicchio di Matelica

Montepulciano /
Trebbiano d'Abruzzo

Locorotondo

Martina Franca

Sálice Salentino

The Marches

*The Castelli di Jesi hills
nourish Verdicchio vineyards and
give their name to a well-known
Verdicchio wine.*

ANCONA
**Az. Agr. Dr Mario
Marchetti** Via Pontelungo
166. Tel: 071 897386
(Maurizio and Letizia
Marchetti). All year. t. E.
G. TF. WS. Historic villa
of 1830s.

**CASTELPLANIO
STAZIONE**
**Casa Vinicola Fazi-
Battaglia 'Titulus' SpA**
Via Clementina 175
(Offices: Via XX Settembre
98g, 00187 Roma). Tel: 06
4741041 (Michele
Miglietta). Feb-July, Sept-
Nov. T. E. Fr. TF. WS.

**CIVITANOVA
MARCHE**
**Az. Agr. Fattoria La
Monacesca** Via
d'Annunzio 1. Tel: 0733
72602 (Aldo Cifola). All
year. T. E. TF. WS. Small
groups only.

CUPRAMONTANA
**Colonnara Co-op.
Agricola** Via Mandriole 6.
Tel: 0731 780273 (Signor
Gagliardini). All year
except harvest-time. T. E.
Fr. TF. WS.

**FABRIANO Casa
Vinicola Mecvini** Via
Dante 112. Tel: 0732 21680
(Enzo Mecella). Jan-Dec.
T. E. TF. WS.

JESI
Enoteca Regionale Via
Federico Conti 2.
1600–2000. Closed Sun.
TP.WS.ER.

**For further addresses, see
p.116.**

The best way to travel along the
length of the Adriatic coast is to use
the A14 motorway as a vertical axis,
and only to cut inland as necessary.

Urbino

Coming south from Romagna, the
first diversion will be inland to
Urbino. The vast hilltop Ducal
Palace dates mainly from the mid
15th century, when Federigo da
Montefeltro, a great warrior and a
notable patron of art, ruled Urbino.
The palace has wonderful views over
the countryside, and it contains the
National Gallery of the Marches.

The wines of the area are the white
Bianchello del Metauro and the red
Sangiovese dei Colli Pesaresi – both
are light wines of local interest.

Verdicchio

The best known wine of the Marches
is Verdicchio. There are, in fact, two
Verdicchios; Verdicchio di Matelica
is the rarer one and comes from near
Fabriano; Verdicchio dei Castelli di
Jesi is the well-known one that
comes in the amphora shaped bottle.
Verdicchio is the Muscadet of Italy
– fruity, with a refreshing acidity, to
be drunk young.

The wine is made from the grape
of the same name. As a still wine, it
is capable of more character than its
nearest rivals, Frascati and Soave.
As a sparkling wine, it already has a
long tradition; it may have been
French troops who introduced the
idea to the area at the time of the
Napoleonic Kingdom of Italy.
Certainly there is no better wine to
accompany the local fish and white
meats than crisp, fruity Verdicchio.

The castles of Jesi

The Castelli di Jesi of the Verdicchio
wine appellation are the small hill
towns surrounding Jesi to the North,
South and West. In the times when
the Marches were a troubled border
area these satellite fortified towns
owed allegiance to Jesi, a garrison
town of massive fortifications, with
handicraft and other shops in the
alleys of the old fortifications.

In 1589 Pope Sixtus V decreed that
on the Feast of San Floriano every
year each tribute town should present
a *Pallio*, or standard, to Jesi in a
public ceremony. This obligation
continued until the early 1800s. The
custom is recalled by the top of the
range 'Pallio di San Floriano' wine
made by the Monte Schiavo co-
operative.

Several of the Castelli di Jesi towns
are worth visiting. Local food

110

specialities such as *Tagliatelle alla porchetta* are well suited to Verdicchio. Cupramontana is the acknowledged 'Capital of Verdicchio' and has an International Museum of Wine Labels. Staffolo has superb views over neighbouring hill towns; the church of San Francesco al Musone is reputedly where St Francis halted to pray on his way to Ancona.

North of Jesi there is Morro d'Alba with its own robust red D.O.C. wine, Lacrima di Morro d'Alba. The Utensilia museum displays farming and wine-making implements, and an interesting walk can be had in the 17th-century walkway around the town walls.

The main road from Ancona westwards is signposted 'Roma'. Stop at Fabriano for its Paper Museum and mediaeval town centre, and to taste the wines of Mecvini.

Rosso Conero and Piceno
There are two important red wines in the Marches, both intended for ageing. Rosso Conero comes from Mount Conero just south of Ancona. There is a good opportunity for tasting in July and August at the Mostra in Numana. For a tiny traditional cellar, visit Dr Marchetti's villa near Ancona.

Rosso Piceno Superiore, which can be like a Chianti Riserva, comes from the Tronto valley further down the coast. Don't miss Ascoli Piceno with its wealth of mediaeval and Renaissance buildings, or the pretty hills around Offida where the Strada del Rosso Piceno leads the traveller past several wineries on the way back to the coast.

Urbino's Ducal Palace commands wonderful views over the countryside and contains the National Gallery of the Marches.

The neck label of Rosso Conero (below) features the Roman triumphal arch at Ancona, built by the emperor Trajan.

Abruzzo and Molise

CONTROGUERRA
Az. Vit. Dino Illuminati
Contrada San Biagio 18.
Tel: 0861 856631 (Signor
Agostino). All year. T (only
for groups). G. TF. WS.
Small wine museum in
cellars.

LORETO APRUTINO
Az. Agr. Valentini Via del
Baio 2. Tel: 085 826138
(Edoardo Valentini).
Weekdays, all year. T. TP.
WS. Famous for Trebbiano
d'Abruzzo wine.

ORTONA
**Consorzio Co-operative
Riunite d'Abruzzo 'Vini
Citra'** Contrada Cocullo.
Tel: 085 9195342 (Signor
Cameli). All year. T. E. G.
TF. WS.

TOLLO
Cantina Tollo Soc. Co-op.
Via Garibaldi. Tel: 0871
959726. All year. T (10
days in advance). TF. WS.

TORANO NUOVO
**Az. Agr. Barone
Cornacchia** Loc. Le
Torre. Tel: 0861 82181
(Piero Cornacchia). T. TP.
WS. Weekday afternoons.
Vignaiolo Pepe Via Chiesi
10. Tel: 0861 856493 (Rosa
Pepe). T (weekdays,
preferably afternoons). TP.
WS.

Until the building of the motorway
from Rome, Abruzzo was more or
less cut off from the rest of Italy. Even
today travelling here by train is a
nightmare; there is no direct route.
But if you are driving it is only an
hour by motorway from L'Aquila to
Rome, and the A14 has brought
Abruzzo into the Bologna/Brindisi
axis.

In the 1970s this was definitely
part of the poor Mezzogiorno, the
backward South of Italy. But since
the motorway came the area has
gained new wealth, and Abruzzo now
has the highest per capita income of
the Mezzogiorno.

In wine terms, Abruzzo has the
highest percentage of D.O.C. wines
in southern Italy, but in terms of
quantity it is a long way behind
Sicily and Puglia.

About a quarter of the grape
harvest is for eating. About 7 or 8
per cent of wine production is
D.O.C., but there's not much
incentive to increase this figure; one
of the absurdities of the E.E.C. is
that the grape producer can earn
more from distilling table wine or
selling grapes for eating.

Abruzzo's three wines

In Italian terms it's a relief to come
across a region where there are only
three names to remember.

Montepulciano d'Abruzzo is a
smooth red wine with an attractive
earthy nose, particularly good value;
it can be aged for up to about 10
years. It is made from the
Montepulciano grape (not to be
confused with the Tuscan wine Vino
Nobile di Montepulciano).

If the skins are extracted from the
fermentation process soon after it
has begun, a rosé wine results;

Montepulciano d'Abruzzo
Cerasuolo takes its name from its
cherry-like colour. It is a pleasantly
dry wine and should be drunk when
still young.

The white of the region is
Trebbiano d'Abruzzo. Often the
Trebbiano produces dull and flat
wines. In Abruzzo the whites tend
to be more characterful; Valentini is
the most famous producer.

The wine roads

Abruzzo has the benefits of
mountains, hills and beach resorts
all within a short distance of each
other. Skiing, sight-seeing and
swimming are possible in a single

day. It is in the hills just inland from the sea that the vineyards are to be found.

Just over the border from the Marches, the hilly town of Controguerra has panoramic views over the surrounding countryside. Visit Illuminati's Fattoria Nico for a tasting of some of the best local wines. The nearby town of Torano Nuovo has two other leading wineries worth a visit, Barone Cornacchia and Emidio Pepe.

Atri to Chieti

On your way southwards on the coastal route stop at the hill town of Atri. The town has an ancient past. It has a frescoed cathedral built on Roman foundations; indeed the Adriatic Sea may well derive its name from the town's old Roman name, Hadria Picena.

Inland from Pescara, on the pretty hills of Loreto Aprutino, are the Valentini vineyards. Edoardo Valentini makes one of Italy's most extraordinary white wines. He ages a

Trebbiano d'Abruzzo in oak casks to produce a wine that lasts at least four years after the vintage year.

Most of the wine in Abruzzo comes from the province of Chieti. Try to visit the town for its Roman remains, and for the archaeological museum with its prize exhibit, the extraordinary 6th-century BC statue known as the *Warrior of Capestrano*. Tollo, a small town towards Ortona, has a co-operative whose wines are excellent. If you like full reds, try their Colle Secco Montepulciano d'Abruzzo.

Molise

Once considered secondary to Abruzzo, Molise has recently gained administrative independence. This is remote and attractively rural countryside, and several traditional industries are still alive here: lace, carpets, ceramics and terracotta, for example.

The two D.O.C. wines of Molise, Pentro and Biferno, are made in similar styles to the wines of Abruzzo.

The town of Celano in Abruzzo with its imposing 15th-century castle bears witness to Abruzzo's military past.

Puglia

Almost one fifth of Italian wine production comes from Puglia, but only about 1.3 per cent is D.O.C.

Traditionally, Puglia has produced powerful red wines, suitable for blending with the quality wines of the North, or even with French wine.

With ever-decreasing consumption of alcohol in Europe the wine producers of Puglia have either relied on Common Market subsidies or they have developed the quality side of the market. There are over 20 D.O.C. *appellations* and several Vini a Indicazione Geografica.

Puglia's wine roads

Travelling south along the A14 Adriatic motorway one of the first towns encountered is Lucera. Lucera reflects the epochs of Puglia's importance with its Roman amphitheatre, Swabian castle and Angevin cathedral. Its wine is a tongue-twister: Cacc'e mmitte di Lucera – the dialect name apparently means 'drink and pour again'.

Puglia is rich in Roman and in early mediaeval history. Near Canosa is Canne della Battaglia, Cannae where Hannibal was defeated by the Romans in 216 BC. Canosa itself has two masterpieces of Puglian art in the 11th century bishop's throne and pulpit in the cathedral.

Rosso Canosa is one of the three local reds: the others are Rosso di Barletta and Rosso di Cerignola. An unusual wine of the area is Moscato di Trani which is a sweet muscat excellent with fruit.

The finest monument to Puglia's Golden Age is the Castel del Monte a few kilometres south-east of Canosa. It was built as a hunting lodge by the Emperor Frederick II

Locorotondo (above) is one of the most splendid 'white towns' of the Puglian plains. It produces its own D.O.C. wine, as does its neighbour Martina Franca.

around 1240 and has a distinctive octagonal design.

Castel del Monte gives its name to the D.O.C. wine whose most famous exponent is the Rivera company in Andria. They are well known for their rosé; their best wine is a Riserva called Il Falcone. Like Favonio in Fóggia they are experimenting with foreign grape varieties.

The *Trulli*

Midway between Bari and Brindisi is Alberobello and the zone of the *trulli*. These conical-roofed peasant dwellings originated as an easy method of house building; the local rocks easily split into thin layers ideal for dry stone wall construction. In the time of the Bourbon rule when new houses were taxable, this construction meant they were easily dismantled if necessary.

Locorotondo, Ostuni, and Martina Franca are the three local whites.

Lecce and Táranto

In the heel of Italy is the lovely Baroque town of Lecce.

Nearby are the D.O.C. wine areas of Sálice Salentino, Leverano and Alezio. The rosé versions are very successful: Rosa del Golfo from Giuseppe Calò and Five Roses from Leone de Castris especially. Five Roses acquired its name during the war when American soldiers apparently rated it more highly than a well-known Bourbon.

Between Lecce and Táranto is Manduria, home of the Primitivo grape that is perhaps the origin of California's Zinfandel. The wine is a formidably strong red which can be sweet and fortified, too.

Táranto is well worth a visit. It was the most important city in the Greek colony of Magna Graecia and has an important archaeological museum.

SALICE SALENTINO Antica Az. Agr. Vit. Leone de Castris Via Senatore de Castris 50. Tel: 0832 731112 (Dr Dino Pinto). All year. T. E. TF. WS. Small wine museum and restaurant Villa Donna Lisa (tel: 0832 732222).

Harvesting in the vineyards around Locorotondo. The local co-operative is responsible for the international fame of its uncomplicated white wine.

Food and Festivals

FURTHER INFORMATION

Assessorato al Turismo della Regione Puglia Ente Provinciale per il Turismo, Via Monte S Michele 20, 73100 Lecce. *Apulia – guide to sightseeing and good eating*, a free guide published by Istituto Geografico de Agostini, is available here.
Aziende Autonome di Soggiorno S. Benedetto del Tronto. Tel: 0735 2237/ 4115. Information on wine road tours.
Camera di Commercio I.A.A. di Ancona Piazza XXIV Maggio I, 60124 Ancona. Tel: 071 29446.
Ente di Sviluppo nelle Marche Via Alpi 20,60100 Ancona. Tel: 071 8081.

FURTHER ADDRESSES

THE MARCHES

LORETO
Casa Vinicola Giocchino Garofoli C.P. 25. Tel: 071 970218. All year. T. TF. WS.

MACERATA
L'Enoteca Via Catenati 2. Tues-Sat 1700–2000. TP. WS. EP. Public Enoteca of the Province of Macerata.

MONTE SCHIAVO DI MAIOLATI SPONTINI
Co-op. Vin. Prod. Verdicchio Monte Schiavo Via Vivaio. Tel: 0731 700297 (Rolando Spadini, Mauro Bambini). All year. T. E. Fr. TF. WS.

OFFIDA
Villa Pigna dei Fratelli Rozzi Contrada Ciafone. Tel: 0736 87239 (Signor Pasqualino Gabrielli). All year. T. E. G. Fr. TF. WS.

FOOD SPECIALITIES

The Marches
The cuisine of the Marches is ingenuous and uncomplicated; dishes are cooked in a simple, healthy manner. Some specialities:
Brodetto: fish stew, traditionally with as many fish as there are apostles, except that none of the 12 is bad.
Vincisgrassi: owes its name to an Austrian prince who stopped in Ancona in Napoleonic times, Prince Windisch-Gratz; baked lasagne with chicken liver and white sauce.
Stoccafisso all'Anconitana: stewed stockfish.
Tripe from Jesi, *Tripa alla canapina*.
Game from Loreto.
Salami from Fabriano.

FESTIVALS

Marches
Easter Monday: SAN MARCELLO: sausage and salami festival.
May: MONTECAROTTO: fish and Verdicchio festival.
First Sunday of June: SAN MARCELLO: Palio Sanmarcellese, folk festival.
July and August: NUMANA: Rosso Conero and Verdicchio exhibition.
First Sunday of August: STAFFOLO: festival.
August: PESARO: Rossini Festival.
August: ROSORA: festival of Verdicchio.
September: ASCOLI PICENO: Giostra della Quintana: mediaeval joust and Renaissance costume procession.
Last Sunday of September: ARCEVIA: *festa dell'uva*.
First Sunday of October: CUPRAMONTANA: *festa dell'uva* and wine exhibition.

Olive ripiene all'ascolana: large stuffed and deep fried green olives

Abruzzo Molise
The most famous dish of Abruzzo is *Maccheroni alla chitarra*, made by stretching a thin sheet of fresh pasta over a frame with wires like guitar strings that cuts the pasta into strips. The sauce is meat or tomato based.

Like all the Adriatic coastal regions there is a version of *brodetto*, fish soup, adapted to the local catch. Fish is regarded more highly than meat in this region.

The traditional cheese used to flavour pasta dishes is often pecorino (sheep's cheese) rather than parmesan. It goes especially well with lamb and vegetable-based sauces.

Abruzzo Molise
January: RIVISONDOLI: Presepe Vivente, nativity scene.
Easter: L'AQUILA: Good Friday Procession.
Easter Sunday: SULMONA: '*Madonna che scapa in piazza*' procession.
May, first Thursday: COCULLO: procession of the Serpari in which a statue of St Dominic is paraded adorned with live snakes.
August: MONTEPAGANO: wine festival.
August: ORTONA: Rassegna Regionale dei Vini, regional wine festival.
August: BASCIAMO: prosciutto festival.
September: ORTONA: mullet festival.

Puglia
May: BARI: feast of St Nicholas procession recalls the arrival of the bones of the Saint in 1087.
September: MASSAFRA: Palio della Mezzaluna, celebrates a battle against the Saracens.

Some specialities:

Orecchie di preti: priests' ears pasta.

Scripelle imbussi: pancakes filled with cheese and ham.

Trippa alla paesana: tripe with hot peppers and tomatoes.

Puglia

The cuisine of Puglia is based on simple products and strong flavours. The most famous pasta of Puglia are the ear-shaped *orecchiette*.

The coast provides fresh fish and shellfish: anchovies, mussels, squid and oysters particularly.

Lamb is very important, reflecting the fact that Puglia is the third most important region for sheep farming after Lazio and Sardinia.

Some specialities:

Annulieddu a lu furnu (Agnello al forno): baby lamb and potato casserole.

Calzengfiidde: small calzone, or pizza envelope filled with meat or cheese.

Ciambotto: pasta sauce made of tiny fish with onions and tomatoes.

Cozze gratinate: baked mussels.

Melanzane ripiene: stuffed aubergines.

Peperoni arrotolati: stuffed peppers.

Zuppa di pesce alla gallipolina: fish stew with a little tomato and vinegar.

Tourism has become important for the trulli *– conical-roofed peasant dwellings – in Alberobello (see page 114) at Locorotondo.*

OSTRA VETERE
Az. Agr. Fratelli Bucci
Via Cona 30. Tel: 071 96179 (Dario Carbini). T. TF. WS. Maximum 10 visitors.

STAFFOLO
Az. Agr. Fratelli Zaccagnini Via Solferino 14. Tel: 0731 77119. All year. T. TF. WS.

The Mediterranean Coast

The further south you travel the deeper you are in the Mezzogiorno, Italy's most poverty-stricken and depressed region. This is the home of those who have perfected the *arte di arrangiarsi*, the art of getting by, by hook or by crook. It is no accident that Naples, with its high unemployment, has a thriving underground economy, and horrifying crime levels. Yet this is a city packed with wonderful churches, Roman, mediaeval and Baroque, and with a glorious ancient past still manifest in its ruins and museums. (Rome is untypical; ancient, proud and bureaucratic, with great treasures and impossible traffic.)

Four regions are involved. Lazio is divided by Rome, south of which the Mezzogiorno begins. Campania's salvation is the tourism of Naples, Capri, Ischia and the Amalfi coast. Basilicata, in the instep of Italy, is very poor. Calabria's hope and challenge is the tourism the motorways bring.

The Spanish Steps in Rome, one of countless monuments to the city's Baroque splendour. Locals drink the fresh white wines of the Colli Albani.

Lazio

Until the beginning of the present century, Rome was surrounded by deserted and malaria-ridden countryside, except for the Colli Albani hills to the south-east. Here, amidst the summer villas of the Roman aristocracy, the predominantly white wines of the region are produced. Frascati is most famous, but each hill town has its own wine. Some are D.O.C.: Marino, Montecompatri and Velletri, for example, as well as Frascati. These are clean and simple wines; if they have any striking feature it is the bitter almond twist to the aftertaste.

Wine is also made north of Rome, around Cervéteri, and between the Colli Albani and the coast, on the plains drained by Mussolini near Aprília. The Merlot of Aprília can be very good.

Campania

The resorts of Capri and Ischia produce their own wines, of local interest only. From vineyards around

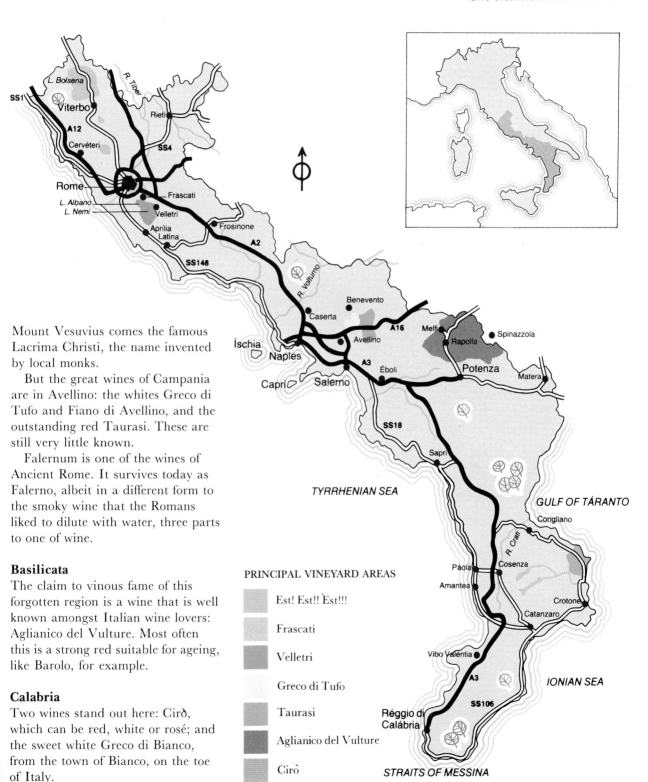

Mount Vesuvius comes the famous
Lacrima Christi, the name invented
by local monks.

But the great wines of Campania
are in Avellino: the whites Greco di
Tufo and Fiano di Avellino, and the
outstanding red Taurasi. These are
still very little known.

Falernum is one of the wines of
Ancient Rome. It survives today as
Falerno, albeit in a different form to
the smoky wine that the Romans
liked to dilute with water, three parts
to one of wine.

Basilicata

The claim to vinous fame of this
forgotten region is a wine that is well
known amongst Italian wine lovers:
Aglianico del Vulture. Most often
this is a strong red suitable for ageing,
like Barolo, for example.

Calabria

Two wines stand out here: Cirò,
which can be red, white or rosé; and
the sweet white Greco di Bianco,
from the town of Bianco, on the toe
of Italy.

PRINCIPAL VINEYARD AREAS

Est! Est!! Est!!!

Frascati

Velletri

Greco di Tufo

Taurasi

Aglianico del Vulture

Cirò

Frascati

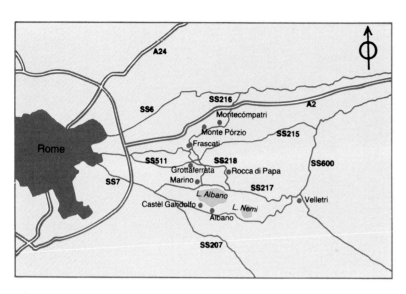

MONTE PORZIO CATONE

Cantine Colli di Catone SpA Via Frascati 31/33. Tel: 06 9449113 (Antonio Pulcini). All year except Aug-Oct. T. E. TF. WS. Minimum 5 visitors.

Cantine San Marco snc Via di Frascati 60. Tel: 06 9422689 (Umberto Notarnicola). All year except Aug. T. TP (at Osservatorio restaurant next to Cantina). WS.

Fontana Candida Via di Fontana Candida 11. Tel: 06 9408313 (Francesco Bardi). All year except Aug. T. E. G. TF. WS.

The wines of Lazio in general do not have a strong character; they are quite unlike the masculine, opaque reds of Piedmont or the delicate feminine wines of the Veneto. Instead, the whites of Lazio, and its few reds, are impersonal; too often in a Roman trattoria or a less exalted restaurant they are poured into a jug from a carefully-hidden 2-litre bottle, which may not be from Lazio – it could be full of Sicilian wine. It's best to ask for a bottle, and check that it is not too old; you may then pay twice as much but you will almost certainly drink more happily.

Frascati

For 2,000 years the Castelli Romani hills south-east of Rome have been the recreational resort of the Romans. Cicero had a villa at Tuscolo, and tradition has it that Cato lived at Monte Pórzio Catone. Colli di Tuscolo and Villa di Catone are wine brands that recall this heritage. It's a delightful area, but try to avoid the Roman holidays. It's still possible to find the traditional rustic *osteria*, where pitchers of local wine can be

enjoyed outside at a table sheltered from the sun that Rome seems to bask in for much of the year. Here wine is to be drunk for enjoyment, not to be analysed.

Frascati is the name that everyone recognizes. It is a clean, but slightly rich tasting pale white, with a touch of almond flavour on the aftertaste. It must be drunk young, no older than two vintages.

Frascati the place is one of a semi-circle of towns around the Colli Albani hills. The hills are, in fact, extinct volcanoes, and the two lakes, Albano and Nemi, are water-filled craters. Lake Nemi was known as the Mirror of Diana in classical times, because of the pagan temple sited on its shores.

The town of Frascati is almost a suburb of Rome, but its splendid villas witness the popularity it enjoyed as a retreat for the Roman aristocracy. Villa Aldobrandini and the monument to Bonnie Prince Charlie in the cathedral of San Pietro are worth seeing.

Wines of the Colli Albani

Frascati is only one of the wines produced in the Colli Albani area, also south-east of Rome. The others, all whites with pretty similar characteristics, are Marino, Colli Albani, Colli Lanuvini, Montecompatri Colonna, Velletri and Zagarolo. Velletri, unusually, is also made as a quaffable red wine that is usually very good value.

Using the side roads, it is a pleasant drive to turn off the A2 motorway at Monte Pórzio Catone, where many of the Frascati producers are based, and then follow the roads around the Colli Albani hills to Velletri.

Grottaferrata, Castèl Gandolfo

Grottaferrata has panoramic views and an 11th-century Byzantine abbey. Marino is a little town above the shores of Lake Albano, and its wine is next to Frascati in popularity.

Just around the shores of the lake is Castèl Gandolfo, the Pope's famous private residence and ancient site of Alba Longa.

An elaborate sculpted fountain (left) at Frascati, near the town hall.

Not far from Frascati is the Abbey of San Nilo (below) at Grottaferrata.

Aprília

Between the Colli Albani hills and the coast are the plains of Aprília. They claim that the Trebbiano, Merlot and Sangiovese di Aprília should be excellent, as the climate is similar to California's. My own favourite is the fruity red Merlot.

Anagni

On the A2, about 20km (12 miles) before Frosinone, Anagni has a superb Romanesque cathedral as well as Cesanese del Piglio, an unusual red in several styles: dry for long ageing; *amabile* (medium sweet); and *dolce* (sweet).

ROME

Enoteca Trimani Via Goito 20. Tel: 06 497971. Daily 0900–1300, 1600–2000. Marco Trimani is one of the greatest publicists of wine.

Campania

Campania has two faces: one is the traditional jolly image of Italy, spaghetti and pizza, holidays on Capri and Positano, gaiety, dance and song. The other face is the high unemployment of Naples, the viciousness of its Mafia, the Camorra, and the extensive destruction still evident from the 1980 earthquake.

Classical wines of Campania

Wine in this land has a very ancient tradition. The Greeks who colonized southern Italy before Roman times were so struck with the vine-growing potential here that they called their colony Enotria, which comes from Greek *oinos*, which also gives us the word 'wine'. Ischia, whose wine was awarded the first D.O.C. in Campania, was once known as Enaria, 'the land of wine'.

The Greek tradition lingers today in several wine names: Greco di Tufo, Greco di Somma, Vino Greco; and the major red wine grape of Campania and Basilicata called Aglianico derives from *hellenico*, 'the Greek one'.

The ancient Romans loved the wine Falernum, and it was made to withstand long ageing. In fact, the Romans were sophisticated in their treatment of wine, and used both corks and glass bottles. Tiberius is said to have had the inventor of an allegedly unbreakable glass put to death, for fear of ruining the economy.

In praise of Falernum

Legend has it that Bacchus, in disguise as a poor man, asked a peasant near Mount Massico for some refreshment. The peasant was so generous that Bacchus turned his homely milk into a wonderful wine

– and Falernum was the peasant's name.

Virgil, Horace and Martial praised the wine's virtues. Martial wrote the following lines: 'Livia five, Giustina eight, Licia and Lidia five and four, Ida three. As many letters as I have sent my lovers so I've poured cups of Falernum. And since none of them has come to me; come, sleep, to me.'

The new Falerno is made just over the border from Lazio into Campania, where Fattoria Villa Matilde make both red and white Falerno. The red Riserva is particularly successful.

Around Naples

The two islands off the Gulf of Naples, Ischia and Capri, each produce their own red and white wines. They are not worth taking back to the mainland, but there is nothing wrong with them in their own setting.

Vesuvius is the site of vineyards that grow the Lacrima Christi (meaning 'Tear of Christ') del Vesuvio. This red, white and rosé wine is mainly famous for its name, but in the hands of a good producer such as Mastroberardino, it is respectable enough.

Campania's top wines

There are at present only seven D.O.C. wines in Campania: Ischia (red and white), Taurasi (red), Greco di Tufo (white), Solopaca (red and white), Capri (red and white), Fiano di Avellino (white), Vesuvio (red and rosé, Lacrima Christi del Vesuvio, white).

This is a small list considering the fame of the area in classical times. Re-discovery is overdue.

In the hinterland behind Naples

are the best wines of Campania. A turning off the A16 motorway leads to Atripalda, where Mastroberardino has its cellars. If anyone deserves the credit for the fame of the wines of this area abroad, it is Antonio Mastroberardino, who has put these otherwise obscure wines on the map.

Fiano di Avellino and Greco di Tufo are the whites. The red is called Taurasi after the Roman town of Taurasia by the banks of the river Calore. It is made of the Aglianico grape and capable of great ageing, like its rival, Aglianico del Vulture, further south in Basilicata.

Steeply terraced vineyards on the Amalfi coast produce wines of mainly local interest.

Basilicata and Calabria

POTENZA
Enoteca Lucana Via
Cairoli 7. Tel: 0971 37083.
0900–1300, 1700–2100.
Closed Thurs p.m.

REGGIO DI CALABRIA
Enoteca Tripodi Via
Veneto 46a. Tel: 0965
95009. 0900–1300,
1630–2000. Near the
museum of the Riace
bronzes.

RIONERO
**D'Angelo Fratelli Casa
Vinicola** Via Provinciale
8. Tel: 0972 721517
(Donato d'Angelo). All
year except Nov and Dec.
T. E. TF. WS. Near castle
of Frederick II.

Called Lucania under the pre-war
Fascist government, Basilicata only
acquired its present name in 1947.

This remote region is movingly
described in Carlo Levi's famous
autobiographical story *Christ Stopped at
Eboli*. Eboli itself is in Campania,
but Levi's experience was of
Basilicata, where he was 'exiled' by
the Fascists, and indeed he is buried
there. His painting *Lucania 1961* is on
display at the Centro Levi in Matera.
In any case, don't miss the Sassi area
of Matera where dwellings and
churches cut into the rock have been
occupied since prehistoric times.

Basilicata wines
Only one wine is D.O.C. and in the
league of great Italian wines:
Aglianico del Vulture. This red wine
is made in several versions: Riserva
(five years old), Vecchio (three years
old), Spumante (sparkling), and
Dolce (a sweet dessert wine).

Aglianico is made in the northern
tip of Basilicata in the area around
Mount Vulture. Visit Fratelli
d'Angelo in Rionero; they are
amongst the best producers of
Aglianico.

Calabria
The deep southern toe of Italy has its
economic and social problems. Until
recently, emigration from Calabria
was the usual course for its young
people.

However, the discovery of the
spectacular Bronzes of Riace,
ancient sculptures found on the sea
bed off the coast of Calabria, has
done much to restore local pride; they
are now one of the best reasons to
visit the town of Reggio di Calabria.
But despite the new motorways that
are finally bringing in tourist
revenue, you can't expect things to
work smoothly in Calabria, and the
train service is particularly poor.

Ancient Calabrian wines
Little wine is of more than local
interest. Cirò has recently acquired
a good reputation as an
uncomplicated red, white or rosé. It
comes from the town on the western
coast of Calabria, and can claim to
be one of the oldest wines in the
world. When southern Italy and
Sicily was part of Magna Graecia, the
Cremissa wine of this area was
awarded to victorious Olympic
athletes.

Further down the coast, almost on
the toe of Italy, is the town of
Bianco. Greco di Bianco and
Mantonico di Bianco are two dessert
white wines with ancient origins and,
supposedly, strong aphrodisiac
qualities. Visit the area for its
archaeological heritage too – nearby
Locri has impressive Greek temple
remains.

Food and Festivals

FESTIVALS

February 19: NAPLES: feast of San Gennaro; liquefaction of the blood.
Easter: CATANZARO, NOCERA TERINESE, PROCIDA: Good Friday processions.
May: POTENZA: Cavalcade of the Turks.
July: MATERA: Materano Arts Festival.

FOOD SPECIALITIES

Lazio

Sheep farming was once more important than agriculture to the inhabitants of Lazio. *Abbacchio* is milk-fed spring lamb; *Scottadito* (literally 'finger-burner') is grilled cutlets; *Brodettato alla Romana* is a lamb stew with a sauce flavoured with lemon and thickened with egg.

Lazio is also the home of several internationally famous dishes: *Spaghetti alla carbonara* – with diced bacon, egg yolk and parmesan; *Spaghetti all' Amatriciana* – with tomatoes, bacon, onion and garlic; *Saltimbocca* – beef olives with sage and *prosciutto* (raw ham); and *Stracciatella* – consommé, beaten egg and cheese.

Rice is not used, except for the curiously named dish *Supplí al telefono*, rice croquettes filled with mozzarella, whose stringiness provides the reference to telephones.

Campania

Naples is the home of spaghetti and of pizza. Both of these foods are essentially peasant foods and the sauces and toppings tend to be much as they were intended to be: simple. The *Spaghetti al pomodoro* tends to have a typical slightly watery sauce.

The best pizzas are cooked in an open wood-fired oven (look for the sign '*forno a legno*'); a *calzone* is a pizza envelope with a filling rather than a topping; *Pizza alla Napoletana* has a topping of anchovies, tomatoes, and mozzarella flavoured with basil and oregano.

Basilicata: cheese and peppers

From classical times, ancient Lucania has been known for its cheeses: *Provola*, *Caciocavallo* and *Scamorze* are good examples.

The cooking is based very much on local vegetables. Hot and sweet peppers, aubergines, beans, pulses, and lentils, which are cooked in olive oil and flavoured with herbs – these are the essential ingredients.

Calabria

The rites of preserving vegetables are still observed in Calabria. Aubergines, olives, tomatoes and mushrooms all benefit from the southern sun.

Fish, especially trout (*trota*) and swordfish (*pesce spada*), and lamb are also popular. Pasta has many shapes, each with its local name.

FURTHER INFORMATION

Azienda Autonoma Soggiorno e Turismo del Tuscolo Piazza Marconi 1, 00044 Frascati. English translation of the booklet *Itinerari Tuscolani* available.
Consorzio Tutela Vini D.O.C. Frascati Via Matteotti 12/a, 00044 Frascati. Tel: 06 9420022.
Ente Provinciale di Turismo Via de Viti de Marco 9, 75100 Matera. *Basilicata: handbook for the tourist with road map* and *Matera and Province, Tourist itineraries* available.

An Enoteca in Rome displays fine champagnes as well as Italian wines. Champagne and whisky are both surprisingly popular in Italy, which is the largest market for malt whisky in the world.

125

The Islands

Sicily has always been the property of some other nation. Greeks, Phoenicians, Romans, and Goths, then Byzantines, Moors, Normans and Swabians, French, and Spaniards have held sway over the island from one age to another. And today the activities of the Mafia make it hard to integrate the island with the mainland. The Temple of Apollo and Artemis in Syracuse is Sicily's history in microcosm: built by the ancient Greeks, subsequently it became a Byzantine church, a Saracen mosque, a Norman church and a Spanish barracks.

Palermo, the capital, has Norman and Baroque monuments, and a mediaeval palace with glittering mosaic decoration; the northern coast also has Cefalù, a seaside town with a magnificent Norman cathedral. Messina was destroyed in 1908 after an earthquake, and by the Allies in 1943. Taormina's classical remains, clinging to the cliffs beneath Mount Etna, are spectacular. And Agrigento's Temple of Concord is the best preserved Greek temple in Italy.

Once part of Magna Graecia, Sicily's Greek heritage is extensive. The theatre at Taormina, with its view over the coast, dates back to the 3rd century BC.

Sicily should be better known for its wine than it is now. Together with Puglia it is the largest producer of wine in Italy. But only about 2 per cent of this production is D.O.C. and

Sicily is the biggest contributor to the Common Market wine lake.

E.E.C. subsidies and government grants, especially the subsidies from the government for the creation of

wine co-operatives, have meant that the Sicilian wine industry has been able to produce ever-increasing amounts of technically correct wine. No longer are the whites golden, oxidized and undrinkable; no longer do the reds taste like a mixture of baked fruit juice and alcohol. The whites are now clean and crisp, the reds fruity and balanced with the classic hot taste of southern Italy.

But too much wine is produced. There are too few markets for the ordinary quality that the wine represents, and all those subsidies mean that there is little incentive to produce smaller quantities with higher quality.

The safest bet in Sicily is to drink the branded wines: Regaleali, Corvo, Rapitalà, Donnafugata, Cellaro and Settesoli are the names to look for.

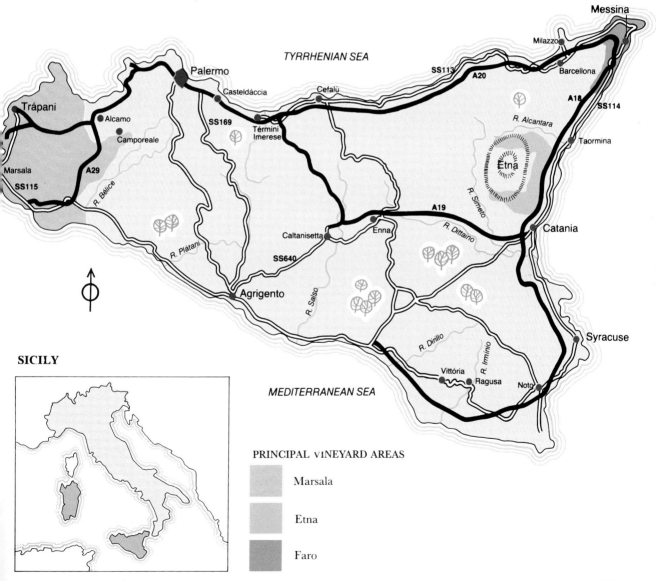

SICILY

PRINCIPAL VINEYARD AREAS

Marsala

Etna

Faro

Sicily and Pantelleria

Most of the important wine producers in Sicily, those with the famous quality-conscious brands, have their wineries in the north-western part of Sicily. Rapitalà, owned by the French count Hugues de la Gatinais, and Regaleali, owned by Conte Giuseppe Tasca d'Almerita, are the aristocratic estates. Corvo is probably the most successful brand; it's an extremely reliable wine found all over the world. Donnafugata is an upmarket red and white whose name comes from the romantic *donna fugata*, 'the woman who fled', a character in Giuseppe di Lampedusa's novel *The Leopard*; the princely villa in the story is on the wine estate.

Wine, however, is produced on all three corners of Sicily, and on the islands of Lipari and of Pantelleria.

Messina and Etna

Just across the Straits of Messina from Calabria is the town of Messina itself. A drive round the *Viali di Circonvallazione*, the ring road, is worthwhile for the splendid views. Heading south on the A18 motorway one drives through the vineyards of the quality red wine called Faro that surround Messina.

Etna has a legendary claim to be the first wine ever created. The young god Bacchus was walking to Sicily, when he stopped to rest on a tree stump, and a mysterious plant grew at his feet. He uprooted it and put it into the hollowed bone of a bird for safe keeping. As he journeyed, it grew so big that he put

The old quarry at Syracuse has a cave known as the Ear of Dionysius. The acoustics are such that the tyrant Dionysius (430–368 BC) is said to have eavesdropped on prisoners from this listening point.

it in a lion bone and finally in an ass's bone. When he reached Nasso, near Taormina, he planted the vine, and it bore fruit. Bacchus picked the grapes and made the first wine. The story has a moral too: a little wine makes you light like a bird, more of it makes you feel like a lion, immoderate use makes you an ass.

Moscato and Cerasuolo

Further down the eastern coast of Sicily visit Catania, and the ancient city of Syracuse, home of Plato and Archimedes.

The Greeks introduced the Moscato grape to Sicily 2,500 years ago. Moscato vineyards and almond trees are a familiar feature of the landscape. Moscato di Siracusa is a rare dessert wine and genuine examples are hard to find. Moscato di Noto, made as a table wine, a sparkling wine and a dessert wine, is commoner.

Just around the southern tip is Vittória where they make a pale but strong rosé called Cerasuolo di Vittória. Unusually for a rosé it can withstand long ageing.

Pantelleria

Midway between Sicily and Tunisia is the beautiful island of Pantelleria. It can be reached by air, or by boat from Trapani, Mazzara or Porto Empedocole on the Sicilian mainland. Its only main road is a picturesque coastal route.

In wine terms, this island, with its active volcanoes and hot springs, is disproportionately famous for its Moscato wine with its own romantic Greek legend. The goddess Thanit, enamoured of Apollo, substituted the wine of Pantelleria for his daily ambrosia, and immediately captured his attention. Indeed, it is the *passito*, sun-dried, grapes that produce the famous dessert Moscato.

CAMPOREALE
Adelkam SpA Vino Rapitalà Contrada Rapitalà (Offices: Via Segesta 9, 91041 Palermo). Tel: 091 332088 (Conte Hugues de la Gatinais). All year Mon-Fri 0900–1130. Closed Aug. t. TF. WS.

CASTELDACCIA
Casa Vinicola Duca di Salaparuta SpA (Corvo) SS113. Tel: 091 953988 (Dr Patrizia Finazzo). Open March-July, Oct-Dec. T. E. Fr. TF. WS.

VALLELUNGA PRATEMENO
Az. Agr. Regaleali Contrada Regaleali. Tel: 0921 52522. Book at: 091 450727 (Marchesa Anna Tasca Lanza). All year except Aug. T. E. Fr. TF. WS. Minimum 18 visitors.

Moscato grapes are laid out to dry in Pantelleria.

Palermo and Marsala

The well-preserved mediaeval mosaics of the Palatina Chapel in the Norman palace in Palermo show Byzantine and Islamic artistic influences.

MARSALA

Az. Agr. Samperi Marco de Bartoli & C. Contrada Fornara Samperi 292. Tel: 0923 962093 (Dr Marco de Bartoli). All year especially summer. T. Fr. TF. WS. Oenological museum in Cantina.

Enoteca Comunale Via Circonvallazione. Tel: 0923 999444. Daily 0800–1200. EP. TF.

Museo della Civiltà Contadina Baglio Biesina, 10km (6 miles) from Marsala on road Marsala-Salemi. Tel: 0923 953057. Country life museum. Daily 0900–1800.

The western tip of Sicily is its most important wine-producing area. The A20 motorway leads the traveller along the northern coast from Messina to Palermo (via Cefalù). The capital city of Sicily has traces of all the foreign powers that have successively dominated the island. Its inhabitants have not yet thrown off their suspicion of foreigners. Beware of *scippatori*, the scooter-riding bag snatchers; it's safer not to take anything valuable with you whilst sightseeing in Palermo.

Alcamo

The wine zone of western Sicily is based around Alcamo. Rapitalà is a superior branded version of this white wine; the winery is at Camporeale about 20km (12 miles) south-east of Alcamo.

The making of Marsala

The story of Marsala dates back to 1773 when John Woodhouse, the son of an English merchant from Liverpool, was driven ashore at Marsala by bad weather on one of his usual trading trips to Italy. It would not have been the first time he had tasted Marsala, but he was sure he could make a profit from shipping it back to England. As was normal at the time, a little spirit was added to preserve the wine on its long voyage back to England, exactly in the same way as Port and Madeira were transported. His first shipment was of 50 pipes (412 litres each), but Woodhouse remained in the port of Marsala to hear from his father in Liverpool what he thought of the wine – the response was enthusiastic and Woodhouse set up in business.

The Woodhouse Baglio, or factory, still stands by the shore in Marsala, but much changed after two centuries of export trade. Other Englishmen soon followed Woodhouse.

Nelson's tipple

Originally there were three rival Marsala companies. Woodhouse's company and the wine were given official approval in 1798 when Nelson ordered his Marsala for the fleet after the battle of Aboukir Bay. He described the wine as 'good enough to be on the table of any gentleman'; the price was 1s 5d per gallon, freight-free to Malta. For a short time Marsala was referred to as 'Brontë-Madeira', after the title Duke of Brontë given to Nelson by the Bourbon government.

The other two companies were Ingham Whitaker & Co, founded by the Yorkshireman Benjamin Ingham in 1812, and Florio, founded by

Vincenzo Florio in 1832. The busts of the three rivals are in the S.A.V.I. Florio museum, all three companies having been taken over by Cinzano before World War II.

Marsala and Garibaldi
Marsala can claim to have influenced the course of history. It was the presence of two English ships in the harbour that prevented the blockading Bourbon fleet from opening fire on Garibaldi as he landed with his famous 1,000 volunteers in 1860.

Garibaldi's subsequent visit to the Florio Marsala winery led to a quality of Marsala being named after him; Garibaldi Dolce is still made today. A plaque commemorating the visit is in the Florio museum.

Marsala today
The making of *zabaglione* would be impossible without Marsala. And that culinary necessity has kept the Marsala industry alive, sometimes to

the detriment of its image.

Until recently there was a danger that the real wine would become extinct, since it was disappearing into the sea of new mixed drinks; all sorts of versions were sold in the bottle – egg Marsala is perhaps the most notorious.

The future
Marsala is, in fact, as versatile as sherry; it can be an aperitif or a *digestif*, it can be a fortified wine, or aged as a solera sherry.

Two other factors have saved it from extinction. Serious producers have realized that serious quality wines have to be made. Foremost among these is Marco de Bartoli, whose Vecchio Samperi is like an *oloroso* sherry, rich and nutty without being cloying. Secondly, a strict new code of Marsala production was introduced in 1984.

Visit the Enoteca in Marsala for a tasting of modern Marsala.

MARSALA (cont)
Carlo Pellegrino & Co SpA Via del Fante 39. Tel: 0923 951177 (Dr Massimo Bellina). All year except Aug. T. E. Fr. TF. WS.
S.A.V.I. Florio Via Vincenzo Florio 1. Tel 0923 999222 (Dr Franco Attina). All year except Aug. t. Fr. TF. WS. Minimum 15 visitors. The oldest producers, Woodhouse, belong to Florio.

Palermo is famous for its Baroque heritage, which includes the delightful 16th-century Pretoria Fountain.

Sardinia

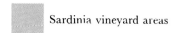

Sardinia vineyard areas

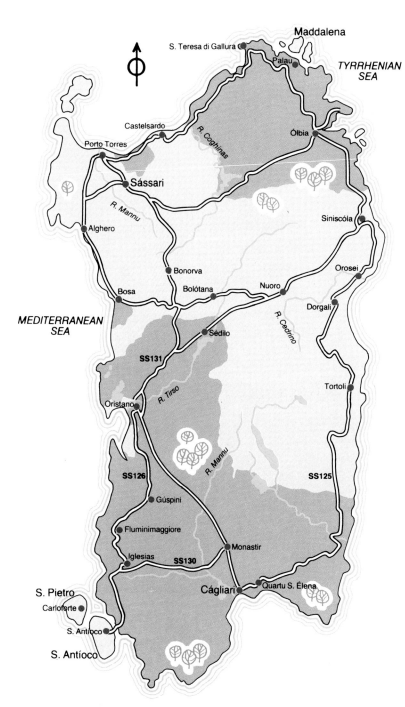

Sardinia is a very separate entity. The fashionable world may alight briefly at the Costa Smeralda on the north-eastern coast, but the Sardinians are still proudly insular, and lack the outward-going nature that gives other Italians of the South such a high profile. Instead, Sardinians are considered almost as mysterious as the neolithic *nuraghi* of their forefathers – round houses that you find throughout Sardinia that are constructed of enormous stones and used variously as fortresses, dwellings and watchtowers.

Sardinian wine tradition

Viticulture in Sardinia has ancient traditions that go back as far as Phoenician times; these middle-eastern traders of biblical times are credited with the introduction of the Nuragus grape to the island. The Spanish domination of Sardinia in the time of the Aragonese kingdom of Naples led to the introduction of Spanish grapes, Cannonau, Monica and Giro, in the 17th century. Sardinian agriculture gained most, however, from the period of the Savoy monarchy, in the 18th and 19th centuries, when immigrants from Piedmont, Liguria and Corsica brought with them new methods of wine-making, and new varieties of vine as well.

Table wines

On the whole, wine production in Sardinia is devoted to table wines of uncertain quality. There are some 39 co-operatives which account for 60 per cent of wine production, but only 4 per cent of all wine produced is D.O.C. There are few companies that export, and consequently few well-known Sardinian wines.

Traditional Sardinian costumes are displayed in Cágliari on the Feast of S. Efisio every year.

ALGHERO
Tenuta Sella & Mosca
Loc. I Piani. Tel: 079 951281 (Giovanni Ortu). T. E. TF. WS.

ARZACHENA
Tenute di Capichera Loc. Capicera. Tel: 0789 81210 (Maurizio and Fabrizio Ragnedda). All year. t. E. WS. TF. Maximum 10 people.

CABRAS
Az. Vin. Contini Attilio
Via Genova 48. Tel: 0783 290806 / 290182 (Antonio Contini). All year. t. E. G. TF. WS. Near archaeological remains at Tharros.

CAGLIARI
Enoteca Cagliaritana
Scalette S. Chiara 21. Tel: 070 655611. 0830–1300, 1600–2000. Closed Sat p.m. and Sun. TP. WS.

JERZU
Società Co-operativa Jerzu Regione su Concali. Tel: 0782 70028. All year 0900–1700. T. TP. WS.

MAGOMADAS
Vignaiolo Arru Emilio & Gilberto Via Sassari 3. Tel: 0785 35319 /35575 (Gilberto Arru). All year. T. Fr. TF. WS.

MONTI
Cantina Sociale del Vermentino Via S. Paolo 1. Tel: 0789 44012 (Dr Sanna). All year. T. TF. WS.

Sella & Mosca

The shining exception to Sardinian anonymity is the Sella & Mosca company of Alghero, on the north-western coast. They are a legacy of the Piedmontese interest in Sardinia; Emilio Sella and Edgardo Mosca were on a hunting holiday here in 1899 when they realized what ideal vine-growing country it was. Now Sella & Mosca is one of Europe's largest wine estates and a temple to modern technology. Their principal wines (none of them D.O.C., but all well made and good value) are the white Vermentino and Torbato and the red Cannonau. They also make a wine that is similar to port called Anghelu Ruju after the famous necropolis north of Alghero.

Other wines and producers

The problem with Sardinian wines is that there is no flagship wine to represent the island. Unlike north Italy, but like much of southern Italy, D.O.C. qualification is not particularly useful – and there are few D.O.C. wines anyway.

Of the co-operatives, that of Dolianova, near Cágliari, produces reliable wines; as does the co-operative of Jerzu, near Nuoro.

Wine names to remember are: (reds) Cannonau, Monica di Sardegna, Carignano del Sulcis; (whites) Malvasia, Moscato (a sweet dessert wine of the Cágliari district), Nuragus, Torbato, and Vernaccia di Oristano (similar to a sherry: rich with a nutty aftertaste).

Food and Festivals

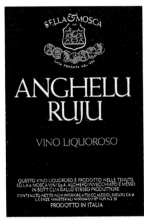

FESTIVALS

Sicily

January 6th: MEZZOJUSO and PIANA DEGLI ALBANESI: colourful Greek Orthodox celebration of Epiphany.
February: AGRIGENTO: almond blossom festival and procession.
February, 3rd and 6th: CATANIA: feast of St Agatha.
Easter: RAGUSA: Procession of the Mysteries, travelling allegories.
July: SYRACUSE: Palio of the Sea – a historical regatta.
July: PALERMO: *U fistinu*, the festival of Santa Rosalia, firework display.
August: MESSINA: Parade of the Giants, commemorating the legendary founding of the city.

Sardinia

January: DORGALI: feast of St Anthony, wine and *pistiddu* (a traditional cake) are offered to public.
February: ORISTANO: the Sartiglia, a costume parade and jousting.
February: BOSA: a carnival.

Easter: SARULE: *S'iscravamentu* – the entire town re-enacts the Deposition.
May: CAGLIARI: Procession of S. Efisio, a costume procession.
May: SASSARI: Cavalcata Sarda, a horseback cavalcade and gallop recalling victory over the Saracens in the year 1000.
June: CALASETTA: Feast of St John the Baptist.
June: CARLOFORTE: Feast of St Peter, decorated boat regatta.
July: EDILO: L'Ardia, a gallop to commemorate Constantine's victory over Maxentius in 312 AD.
August: BONO: a pumpkin festival.
August: NUORO: Feast of the Redeemer, and a folklore festival.
August: GUASILA: Feast of the Assumption.
August: SASSARI: Festival of the Candles, a parade of huge wooden candles, fulfilling a vow made in the plague of 1652.
September: CABRAS: Festival of San Salvatore recalling the defeat of the Saracens.

FOOD SPECIALITIES

Sicily

Sicilian cuisine has two sources: one is the tradition of eastern Sicily around Catania, the other of western Sicily around Palermo. The eastern tradition was established in Sicily 2,000 years ago, when the island had a well-established cooking school. Fortunately, some authentic Sicilian recipes have survived the onslaught of modern tourism:
Pasta cu li sarde: thick spaghetti-type pasta with tomatoes and fresh sardines.
Pasta ca Norma: pasta (spaghetti or penne usually) with tomato sauce, slices of fried aubergine and ricotta, a soft sheep's milk cheese. The dish is a homage to the opera *Norma* (its composer Bellini came from Catania).
Cassata: a mould of ricotta, candied fruit, chocolate, flavoured with Maraschino and vanilla.

Sardinia

The fundamental element in Sardinian food is bread. Bread is baked in a swallowtail shape for baptisms, in garlands for weddings, and brown bread underlines the sadness of funeral feasts. The most

Sicilian puppets representing mediaeval knights and Saracens recall the period of Saracen rule. The Club Palladini, the Sicilian wine-lovers' club, takes its symbol from these traditional puppet figures.

famous product of the Sardinian bakery is *carta da musica*, 'music paper', paper-thin circular sheets of unleavened bread. Its origins lie in peasant cooking, when it was necessary for the shepherd to have something that would keep fresh on his long travels.

Another food of the Sardinian shepherd is cheese. *Cacio fiore* is the most traditional. It can be eaten fresh, grated, or aged with black pepper. Ricotta is called here *gentile*.

Cooking meat on a spit, flavoured with mint, rosemary, bay and sage, is traditional. An alternative is *Carne a carraxiu*: suckling pig is encased in a sheep's stomach and covered with herbs. The parcel is placed in a hole in the ground full of embers and a fire is lit on top. *Porcheddu* is the dialect word for *porchetta*, roast suckling pig.

Is malloredus are Sardinian *gnocchi* (tiny dumplings served as a first course), generally with a tomato or ragù sauce.

Fish is cooked simply. A speciality is the *bottarga* or *buttariga*, smoked mullet or tunny roe.

FURTHER INFORMATION

Azienda Provinciale Turismo Villa Aula, Via Vito Sorba 15, Trápani, Sicily. Tel: 0923 27273.
Camera di Commercio I.A.A. Via Roma 74, Sassari, Sardinia. Tel: 079 276448. Ask for *Sardinia – Island of Wine* (in English and Italian).
Consorzio Volontario per la Tutela del Vino Marsala Palazzo Fiorito, Via Curatolo, 91025 Marsala, Trápani, Sicily. Tel: 0923 953255.
The book *Il Marsala* by Luigi Papo and Anna Pesenti, published by Fabbri in 1986 is available here (in Italian).
Ente Provinciale per il Turismo Piazza Italia 19, Nuoro, Sardinia. Tel: 0784 30083.

Principal Grapes and their Wines

Aglianico (red). Southern Italian grape of great antiquity. Its name derives from *ellenico*, the Greek one. It produces robust reds for long ageing in Basilicata (Aglianico del Vulture) and Campania (Taurasi).

Albana (white). Italy's first white D.O.C.G. is Albana di Romagna, made from this grape in central Italy. The wines are sweet or dry, still or sparkling.

Barbera (red). The staple grape of Piedmont, with Dolcetto. It makes intense reds for drinking within three years, such as Barbera d'Alba, d'Asti, del Monferrato.

Brunello (Sangiovese Grosso) (red). A type of Sangiovese used to make Italy's most prestigious wine, Brunello di Montalcino D.O.C.G.

Cabernet Franc (red). Introduced to north-east Italy in the 19th century, this is widely used to make red wine with grassy characteristics.

Cabernet Sauvignon (red). One of the great grapes of the wine world, little used in Italy (except with unusual wines such as Antinori's Tignanello), sometimes used to give an international flavour to Chianti.

Canonnau (red). This makes one of Sardinia's successful reds, Cannonau di Sardegna.

Chardonnay (white). One of the wine world's most fashionable grapes. Chardonnay from Burgundy produces rich and long-lived white wines. In Italy, it is not generally aged in the same way (in small oak barrels) to achieve the same intensity of flavour and length of ageing. Most Italian Chardonnay is fermented and aged in stainless steel, and therefore has a fresher taste.

Cortese (white). The grape used for Italy's most fashionable white, Gavi, and Cortese dei Colli Tortonesi,
dell'Alto Monferrato, and di Gavi.

Corvina Veronese (red). One of the principal grapes of Valpolicella and Bardolino (together with Rondinella and Molinara).

Dolcetto (red). Piedmont's staple grape, along with Barbera. The name suggests sweetness, but it produces a smooth wine with a slightly bitter aftertaste, often used as a restaurant table wine.

Erbaluce (white). The Piedmontese grape, producing still, sparkling, dry and sweet wines.

Freisa (red). Still, sparkling, sweet or dry wines result from this grape with a characteristic strawberry aroma, from just south of Turin.

Gewürztraminer/Traminer Aromatico (white). Tramin/ Termeno in Alto Adige claims to be the birthplace of this international grape. Used in north-east Italy.

Grechetto (white). The Umbrian grape that gives character to Orvieto.

Grignolino (red). This makes a light red/rosé wine with a slightly bitter aftertaste, from the Asti region.

Lagrein (red). Produces a rosé (*kretzer*) or red (*dunkel*) wine in Alto Adige; light and drinkable wines.

Lambrusco (red). In Emilia Romagna, the wine from this grape is intended to cut the fatty foods of the region. The wine is usually dry, unlike the exported versions.

Malvasia (white). An ancient vine of possibly Greek origins. Malvasia di Candia is one of the major grapes of Frascati, Galestro, Est!Est!!Est!!! and Marino. It is also found extensively in Friuli-Venezia Giulia.

Marzemino (red). This makes a red wine from Trentino celebrated in Mozart's *Don Giovanni*.

Merlot (red). The workhorse grape

of north-east Italy. It makes easy-drinking wines of immediate appeal.

Montepulciano (red). Used on the Adriatic coast to make the red wines Montepulciano d'Abruzzo and Rosso Conero. Not to be confused with the town of Montepulciano in Tuscany which has its own wine, Vino Nobile di Montepulciano made from the Sangiovese grape.

Moscato Bianco (white). One of the great grapes of Italy, this is the source of the fresh grapey tastes of Asti Spumante in Piedmont and Tuscany's Moscadello di Montalcino.

Müller-Thurgau (white). An international grape variety giving a sophisticated but fruity white wine mostly in Friuli-Venezia Giulia and Trentino-Alto Adige.

Nebbiolo (red). The source of two of Italy's best-known and longest-lived wines, Barolo and Barbaresco. Also the base grape for several north-western Italian reds.

Picolit (white). The legendary dessert wine of Friuli, Picolit, is made from the semi-dried grapes of the same name. It is high in alcohol and can be aged for several years.

Pinot Bianco (white). Often confused with Chardonnay by the growers, this grape gives a similar taste to wines mainly made in Friuli and Trentino-Alto Adige.

Pinot Grigio (red). The grape's red skins often give its white wines an attractive pink tinge. The wine has become popular as the thinking skier's white wine. It has good body with a characteristic aromatic twist.

Pinot Nero (red). The best reds of Burgundy are produced from this difficult grape. In north-east Italy it produces light, raspberry-flavoured wines that are highly prized.

Prosecco (white). Versatile grape of the Treviso area of the Veneto. Most popular for the medium dry sparkling wine that is Treviso's house wine.

Riesling (white). The native Italico is less pungent than the Germanic Riesling Renano. Mainly used for varietals in north-east Italy.

Sagrantino (red). An indigenous grape in Umbria, used for red wines with aromas of blackberries and mushrooms.

Sangiovese (red). One of Italy's finest grapes, used in its various forms throughout Central Italy for wines such as Chianti, Vino Nobile di Montepulciano, Brunello and Carmignano (Tuscany), and Rosso Piceno (the Marches).

Sauvignon (white). The grassy green-stick bouquet and flavour of this international grape is less aggressive in Italy than in France.

Schiava/Vernatsch (red). The base grape of the red wines of Trentino-Alto Adige, such as Santa Maddalena, Caldaro and Casteller.

Sylvaner (white). Better known in Alsace, this is also used in Alto Adige to make aromatic white wines.

Tocai Friulano (white). The most common white grape of the eastern Veneto and Friuli-Venezia Giulia.

Trebbiano (white). The grape responsible for most of Italy's white wines, especially Soave, Gambellara, and Frascati.

Verdicchio (white). The versatile white wine grape of the Marches area. It makes still or sparkling wine and can also be aged in small casks.

Verduzzo (white). Produces a white dessert wine from Friuli capable of being aged in *barriques*.

Vernaccia di San Gimignano (white). Responsible for San Gimignano's white wine.

Glossary of Wine Terms

Abboccato slightly sweet; Orvieto Abboccato is the most typical.

Amabile sweet.

Autoclave the tank in which sparkling wine made by the Charmat method (*Metodo Charmat*) gets its sparkle.

Barrique small oak barrel, now fashionable in Italy. Its use gives a smooth initially vanilla flavour.

Bicchiere glass.

Bouquet smell of the wine, resulting from grape, vinification and ageing.

Brillante very clear.

Brut very dry, applied to sparkling wines.

Cantina cellar.

Corpo body and structure of a wine.

Cru single vineyard.

Da bere fresco to be drunk cool.

Degustazione a tasting, the occasion for the **assaggio** (process of tasting).

Denominazione di Origine Controllata (D.O.C.) legal guarantee of origin and of minimum quality of wine. The basic Italian quality indication.

Denominazione di Origine Controllata e Garantita (D.O.C.G.) More rigorous quality control than D.O.C. The wines are assessed by an independent quality control commission.

Dolce very sweet.

Equilibrato balanced.

Erbaceo grassy, especially applicable to Cabernet Franc.

Etichetta label.

Frizzante slightly sparkling.

Fruttato fruity.

Giovane young.

Invecchiamento process of ageing.

Liquoroso wine fortified with added alcohol, such as Marsala.

Metodo Champenois the Champagne method, used for fermentation of sparkling wine in the bottle.

Metodo Charmat method of fermenting sparkling wine in an autoclave (see above).

Millesimato vintage wine.

Morbido smooth and soft.

Neutro without characteristics.

Ossidazione oxidization.

Ossigenazione the process of letting wine breathe, especially desirable for older red wines.

Passito semi-dried grapes which give a rich wine high in alcohol, such as Recioto.

Pieno full, as in full of flavour.

Pigiatura pressing, the first process of wine-making.

Pronta beva to be drunk soon after bottling.

Retrogusto aftertaste.

Robusto a big wine, full of colour, acidity, alcohol and tannin.

Rotondo smooth.

Secco dry.

Spumante sparkling wine. The sparkle can be produced by the *Metodo Champenois* or the *Metodo Charmat* (see above), or by artificially adding bubbles.

Tannico tannin, in a red wine this indicates that it will age well.

Tappo the cork. The same word means 'corked', that is, with a bitter taste given to the wine by a bad cork.

Tastevin small silver tasting bowl used instead of a glass in the cellar.

Tipicità 'typicality', meaning the wine is authentic and traditional.

Uva grape.

Vellutato smooth, velvety.

Vendemmia vintage.

Vigna, vigneto single vineyard.

Vinificazione vinification.

Vino da Tavola table wine.

Vinoso 'like wine', term used especially of a characterless bouquet.

Vivace fresh and often slightly sparkling wine.

Choosing Wine; the Importance of Vintage

White wines

The important rule to remember about most Italian white wines is to drink them as young as possible. This applies to the most common whites, Soave, Pinot Grigio, Frascati and Verdicchio. Generally, white wines of the most recent vintage become available about Eastertime in the following year.

Thus, in 1989 it's best to drink 1987 white wines throughout the year, and 1988 wines towards the end of the year; in 1990, drink 1988 wines throughout the year and 1989 wines towards the end of the year; in 1991, drink 1989 throughout the year and 1990 towards the end of the year, and so on.

The only exceptions to this rule are oak-aged wines such as Frescobaldi's Pomino from Tuscany and Pio Cesare's Pio di Lei in Piedmont. Oak-ageing means that the woody flavours of the oak need several years to blend with the fruit of the grape.

White dessert wines, such as Picolit from Friuli, Vin Santo from Tuscany, and Moscato Passito from Pantelleria are also drunk several years older than the last vintage.

Red wines

There are two types of red wine: the wines for drinking within a year or so of their bottling, such as Valpolicella or Bardolino; and the wines for laying down to mature further in a cellar, such as Barolo and Barbaresco. Some wines can have two versions: Chianti, for example, can be drunk young; Chianti Riserva needs several years' ageing in a cellar.

Red wines for drinking soon

Wines for early drinking include the fashionable *Novello* wines (equivalent to French *Nouveau*), and lighter reds that were not intended for ageing in a cellar. *Drink whatever vintage is generally on sale, but nothing older than five years from the last vintage (three years is normal). The best recent vintage for all red wines is 1988 (1985 was also a vintage year). And avoid 1984.*

CASTELLO di LUZZANO

GUTTURNIO
DEI COLLI PIACENTINI
vino a denominazione di origine controllata

Imbottigliato all'origine dalla
"Azienda Agricola Luzzano" Ziano P.no (Italia)
M. G. FUGAZZA

lt. 0.750 e   PRODUCE OF ITALY   12 % vol.

Red wines for laying down, 1970–85

	Barbaresco	Barolo	Brunello	Chianti Classico Riserva
1970	****	****	*****	****
1971	*****	*****	***	*****
1972	*	*	*	*
1973	**	**	***	**
1974	****	****	**	***
1975	**	**	*****	****
1976	**	**	*	**
1977	**	**	****	****
1978	*****	*****	****	*****
1979	****	****	****	****
1980	****	****	****	****
1981	***	***	***	***
1982	*****	*****	*****	****
1983	****	****	****	****
1984	Avoid	Avoid	Avoid	Avoid
1985	*****	*****	*****	*****

Key to vintage wine chart
Vintages are assessed with star ratings. Five stars indicate an exceptionally good vintage. Remember that vintage wines need several years' ageing in barrel and in bottle before they are released on to the market.

Further Information

Sample letter to an Italian winery

[Sender's name, address and telephone number; date]

La presente per chiedere la prenotazione di una nostra visita alla Vostra stimata cantina.

Abbiamo sentito la fama dei Vostri vini tramite il libro *Travellers Wine Guide – Italy*, nel quale si nota la Vostra gentile disponibilità a dare ai viaggiatori intenditori una visita/degustazione alla cantina. Perciò, siccome siamo molto interessati a sapere di piú sul vino italiano in genere e sul Vostro vino in particolare saremmo molto interessati ad approfittare dell'occasione.

Siamo un piccolo gruppo di [X] persone. Abbiamo intenzione di visitare la Vostra zona i giorni [dates] e chiediamo la Vostra gentile conferma della disponibilità di accoglierci.

Nell'attesa del piacere della Vostra cortese risposta e del piacere dell' eventuale incontro porgiamo i nostri più cordiali saluti,

[signature]

We would like to arrange a visit to your excellent Cantina.

We have heard of the fame of your wines through the publication *Travellers Wine Guide – Italy*, from which we understand that you are willing to accept visits from travellers who are wine lovers and who wish to taste wine in your cellars. We are very interested in learning more about Italian wine in general, and about your wine in particular.

We are a small group of [X] people. We intend to visit your area on the following dates [...] and would be very pleased if you could confirm that you would be able to accept a visit on one of those days.

We look forward to your reply and to the pleasure of meeting you when this can be arranged, with best wishes,

[signature]

Further reading
(in English)
Burton Anderson *Vino*. A standard work on Italian wines, by the leading English-language writer on the subject.

Burton Anderson *The Pocket Guide to Italian Wine*.

Nicolas Belfrage *Life Beyond Lambrusco*. In-depth examination of the current state of wine-making in Italy.

Spike and Charmian Hughes *Pocket Guide to Italian Food & Wine*.

David Gleave *The Wines of Italy*. Well-illustrated guide to Italian wine by grape variety.

Marc and Kim Millon *The Wine Roads of Europe*. Covers Piedmont, the Veneto, Tuscany, Lazio and parts of Friuli with itineraries.

Bruno Roncarati *Viva Vino*. A useful reference work.

Sheldon and Pauline Wasserman *Italy's Noble Red Wines* Comprehensive tasting notes on a wide range of the finer Italian reds.

(in Italian)
Guida all'Italia dei Vini (Touring Club Italiano, 1985) geographic guide to Italian D.O.C.s and D.O.C.G.s. *Guida dell'Ospitalità Rurale* (Agriturist, Corso Vittorio Emanuele 101, Roma) annual publication listing self-catering and hotel holiday possibilities in farms, villas and castles throughout Italy. Trimani, Marco *Guida ai Vini d'Italia* (Editori Riuniti, 1984) a basic dictionary of Italian wine, with preceding notes on vinification. Veronelli, Luigi *Le Cantine di Veronelli* (Giorgio Mondadori, 1989) recommended wine producers with details of which wines to taste on a visit and how to book that visit.

ITALIAN NATIONAL HOLIDAYS

January 1: New Year
January 6: Epiphany.
Easter Monday: (dates vary). April 25: Liberation Day. May 1: Labour Day. August 15: Assumption of the Virgin. November 1: All Saints Day. December 8: Feast of the Immaculate Conception. Christmas Day and Boxing Day.

Local feast days
Shops and businesses are often closed during festivities. The following is a selection only: April 25: Venice. June 24: Florence. Genoa. Turin. June 29: Rome. July 15: Palermo. September 19: Naples. October 4: Bologna. December 6: Bari. December 7: Milan.

Index

Page references in **bold** type indicate the headings of the information panels; those in *italic* type indicate illustrations.

Index

FURTHER ACKNOWLEDGEMENTS

UK
Books: cited on page 140. Periodicals: *Decanter* Magazine, Vintage Guide and Wines of Italy editions.
Dario Modena of Sunshine Wines; Paul Merritt of R. Trestini; Katie Martin of G. Belloni & Co.

Italy
Books: cited on page 140. Periodicals: *Italian Wines & Spirits* and *Civiltà del Bere,* editions with regional profiles.

Almost every regional government and tourist authority has been generous in its assistance, but special thanks are due to the following:
Aosta Regione Autonoma Valle d'Aosta, Assessorato all'Agricoltura
Lombardy Ottorino Milesi of Regione Lombardia, Servizio Provinciale Agricoltura; Consorzio Vini D.O.C. Oltrepò Pavese
Alto-Adige Camera di Commercio IAA of Bolzano
Veneto Carlo Bastogi of U. Vi. Ve.; Ass. Consorzi Vini Vicentini D.O.C.
Friuli Angelo Pighin of Consorzio Tutela Vini D.O.C. del Grave; Centro Regionale Potenziamento Viticoltura e dell'Enologia del Friuli-Venezia Giulia
Emilia Romagna Ente Tutela Vini Romagnoli
Marche Mario Marchetti of Az. Agr. Mario Marchetti
Tuscany Lucia Franciosi of Consorzio del Gallo Nero; Maurizio Botarelli of Ass. Consorzi Vini del Montalcino; Ente Provinciale per il Turismo di Siena; Pasquale di Lena of Enoteca
    Permanente Italica di Siena
Calabria Regione Calabria, Assessorato all'Agricoltura